Cambridge Elements

Elements in Histories of Emotions and the Senses
edited by
Rob Boddice
Tampere University
Piroska Nagy
Université du Québec à Montréal (UQAM)
Mark Smith
University of South Carolina

OUTDOOR SINGING IN MODERN BRITAIN

A Sensory and Emotional History

Abbi Flint
University of Oxford and Newcastle University
Clare Hickman
Newcastle University

Shaftesbury Road, Cambridge CB2 8EA, United Kingdom

One Liberty Plaza, 20th Floor, New York, NY 10006, USA

477 Williamstown Road, Port Melbourne, VIC 3207, Australia

314–321, 3rd Floor, Plot 3, Splendor Forum, Jasola District Centre, New Delhi – 110025, India

103 Penang Road, #05–06/07, Visioncrest Commercial, Singapore 238467

Cambridge University Press is part of Cambridge University Press & Assessment, a department of the University of Cambridge.

We share the University's mission to contribute to society through the pursuit of education, learning and research at the highest international levels of excellence.

www.cambridge.org
Information on this title: www.cambridge.org/9781009615358

DOI: 10.1017/9781009615402

© Abbi Flint and Clare Hickman 2026

This publication is in copyright. Subject to statutory exception and to the provisions of relevant collective licensing agreements, with the exception of the Creative Commons version the link for which is provided below, no reproduction of any part may take place without the written permission of Cambridge University Press & Assessment.

An online version of this work is published at doi.org/10.1017/9781009615402 under a Creative Commons Open Access license CC-BY-NC-ND 4.0 which permits re-use, distribution and reproduction in any medium for non-commercial purposes providing appropriate credit to the original work is given. You may not distribute derivative works without permission. To view a copy of this license, visit https://creativecommons.org/licenses/by-nc-nd/4.0

When citing this work, please include a reference to the DOI 10.1017/9781009615402

First published 2026

A catalogue record for this publication is available from the British Library

ISBN 978-1-009-61535-8 Hardback
ISBN 978-1-009-61537-2 Paperback
ISSN 2632-1068 (online)
ISSN 2632-105X (print)

Cambridge University Press & Assessment has no responsibility for the persistence or accuracy of URLs for external or third-party internet websites referred to in this publication and does not guarantee that any content on such websites is, or will remain, accurate or appropriate.

For EU product safety concerns, contact us at Calle de José Abascal, 56, 1°, 28003 Madrid, Spain, or email eugpsr@cambridge.org

Outdoor Singing in Modern Britain

A Sensory and Emotional History

Elements in Histories of Emotions and the Senses

DOI: 10.1017/9781009615402
First published online: January 2026

Abbi Flint
University of Oxford and Newcastle University

Clare Hickman
Newcastle University

Author for correspondence: Clare Hickman, clare.hickman@ncl.ac.uk

Abstract: This Element brings together historical sources and contemporary experiences to explore the interplay between singing, sociality, body, and meaning in the English landscape over the past century. It explores the connections between air and song and between singing and movement, through the context of the early twentieth century open-air recreation movement. This is supplemented by recent literature on singing and wellbeing, and the experiences of a contemporary walking choir captured via interviews in the field. The authors argue that outdoor singing has been part of co-constructed soundscapes of the modern English leisure landscape, and ask what this meant for those who participated in collective open-air singing and rambling. They explore how open-air singing connected with conceptions of the countryside, with a sense of fellow-feeling, and how this might have both reified and challenged normative ways of being in landscapes. This title is also available as Open Access on Cambridge Core.

Keywords: Sensory Studies, History of Emotions, Landscape History, History of Medicine, Environmental History

© Abbi Flint and Clare Hickman 2026

ISBNs: 9781009615358 (HB), 9781009615372 (PB), 9781009615402 (OC)
ISSNs: 2632-1068 (online), 2632-105X (print)

Contents

Introduction   1

1 Sensing and Feeling the Landscape via the Body   7

2 Fellow-Feeling through Song   22

3 Relating to Place   36

4 Contemporary Connections and Resonances   55

   Bibliography   66

Introduction

An anonymous writer, evocatively described in 1911 a September night of open-air singing around a campfire following an evening walk where dusk had fallen. Like many, they had their account published in *Comradeship*, the magazine of the Cooperative Holidays Association (CHA):

> A roaring camp- fire – surrounded by scarlet blankets that added materially to the comfort of the evening – and copper-red faces! ... 'Friendship' was never sung with more feeling ... Our London Trio charmed the circle with their lovely 'Lagoon Song,' the swell and cadence fitting delightfully the fire flames, the whisper of the wind and the beck's bright flowing chatter ... mirth and song illumined the mind as the flare-torches of dead gorse lighted the gipsy band.[1]

The singing of the song 'Friendship' from the CHA's own song book highlights the role of fellowship which the organisation saw as a key feature along with the sensory elements of a roaring fire, scarlet blankets, flickering light and the human voice intermingling with natural sounds of wind and water. The experience of darkness may have played a role here too, opening up new kinds of socialities and bringing non-visual senses to the fore in a way that can evoke different ways of connecting with place and other people.[2] This was clearly both an evocative emotional and sensory moment in time captured in words and one which points towards the key themes that we will be discussing within this Element: singing, sociality, the body and place. These intersect environmental, health, social and cultural histories, highlighting the complex interactions involved in outdoor singing within group settings over time.

Open-air singing as an activity highlights the interactions between bodies, places, groups of people and other species, as well as a subject that brings to the fore cultural and social contexts. In this Element we bring together sensory and emotional history approaches to enable insight into the ways in which open-air singing has been practiced and experienced both in the past and in the present; through the open-air singing practices and experiences of outdoor recreation groups and organisations based in the north of England in the early twentieth century. This work emerged from historical research into the development, use, and experience of public paths and trails in the twentieth and twenty-first centuries.[3] Ben Harker has highlighted that open-air singing was already part of rambling culture and actions to open-up access to the countryside in the

---

[1] Anon, 'A Holiday Experience', *Comradeship*, 5:1 (September 1911), 16.
[2] Tim Edensor, 'Reconnecting with Darkness: Gloomy Landscapes, Lightless Places', *Social & Cultural Geography*, 14: 4 (2013), 446–465. https://doi.org/10.1080/14649365.2013.790992.
[3] See www.allourfootsteps.uk/ for more about this UK Arts and Humanities Research Council funded research project.

1930s, in his work on the folk singer Ewan MacColl.[4] Whilst this provides a political lens on the links between open-air singing and rambling, this intersection is underexplored from a sensory and emotional historical perspective.

Our key historic sources are publications from the Sheffield Clarion Ramblers (SCR), the co-operative holiday movement (incorporating both the CHA and the Holiday Fellowship [HF]) both of which were active in the early twentieth century and had strong connections with the countryside around the urban centres of Manchester and Sheffield. Our geographic focus is chosen in part because of the historical importance of these landscapes of open-air leisure and recreation for people from these cities. Where appropriate, we have also used supporting material from other, like-minded groups, involved in open-air recreation during this period. Although different in their backgrounds and formation, many of these groups shared a focus on providing meaningful leisure activities for primarily urban working-class men and women (and sometimes younger folk) as a means of personal and social transformation through rational recreation, connecting with nature and immersion in the countryside.[5] Communal outdoor singing within the landscape (often whilst rambling) was integrated within these groups' activities. To facilitate this, they published individual songs in their regular publications for members, and collated songs into books of lyrics and music available to purchase (see Figure 1).[6]

These archival sources, however, are limited in drawing out some of the more personal narratives of the physical experience of singing in these places; therefore, we supplement these with contemporary experiences of collective singing and rambling in landscapes drawn from new qualitative research with a choir who integrate rural and suburban walking within their practice. One of us (Flint) joined the choir on one of their outings for a go-along interview in 2023 – a mobile method which focuses on talking whilst moving in and through environments and aims 'to (re)place the researcher alongside the participant in

---

[4] Ben Harker. '"The Manchester Rambler": Ewan MacColl and the 1932 Mass Trespass', *History Workshop Journal*, 59 (Spring 2005), 219–28. JSTOR, www.jstor.org/stable/25472794.

[5] Douglas Hope, 'The Democratisation of Tourism in the English Lake District: The Role of the Co-Operative Holidays Association and the Holiday Fellowship', *Journal of Tourism History*, 8: 2 (2016), 105–126. Ann Holt, *G.H.B. Ward 1876–1957: His Lifelong Campaign for Access to the Countryside* (London: The Ramblers' Association, 1985). David Prynn, 'The Clarion Clubs, Rambling and the Holiday Associations in Britain since the 1890s', *Journal of Contemporary History*, 11 (1976), 65–77. Harvey Taylor, *A Claim on the Countryside: A History of the British Outdoor Movement* (Edinburgh: Edinburgh University Press, 1997).

[6] See, for example, George Herbert Bridges Ward, *Songs for Ramblers to Sing on the Moorlands* (Sheffield: Sheffield Clarion Ramblers, 1922); The Holiday Fellowship, *Songs by the Way* (London: Holiday Fellowship, n.d.); The Co-operative Holiday Association and The Holiday Fellowship, *Songs of Faith, Nature and Fellowship* (London: CHA and HF, 1951).

Figure 1 The cover of Ward, G H.B., *Songs for Ramblers to Sing on the Moorlands* (Sheffield: Sheffield Clarion Ramblers, 1922), featuring an illustration of a pair of walking boots.
Credit: Image courtesy of Sheffield City Archives (RefNo. Local Studies Library 784.6 SST).

the context of the 'doing' of mobility'.[7] There are, of course, clear differences between the experiences of people in the early twentieth century to those in the twenty-first. We are aware that the historical, political, social and cultural contexts as well as the demographics of these groups will be different so we are not suggesting that these experiences will be the same, but rather we aim to bring them into conversation with each other to consider broader questions

---

[7] Justin Spinney, 'Close Encounters? Mobile Methods, (Post)phenomenology and Affect', *Cultural Geographies*, 22: 2 (2015) 231–246, p. 232.

about bodily movement, singing and interactions with the environment and other people/other species within the landscape over time.

To provide a wider scholarly context for the central register of sound as a sensory category of analysis, we also position our work within a phenomenological understanding of how people experience and construct meaning with the landscapes which comprise their worlds. As Christopher Tilley has stated, these engagements and understandings are 'grounded in the body itself'.[8] Being and moving in landscapes, from a phenomenological perspective, is multi-sensory, affective, cognitive and embodied.[9] Thus, our perceptions of landscape are both mediated and co-constructed through our bodies: 'we are both in it and of it, we act in relation to it, it acts in us'.[10] Within this we experience senses altogether rather than consecutively; we simultaneously see, hear, smell and feel aspects of environments. The ethnographer Dara Culhane has noted that 'attention to sensory experience invites us to re-imagine our minds and bodies, ideas and feelings, not as binaries that are separate from and opposed to each other but rather as actively living in perpetual and dynamic interaction with each other.'[11] The singing practices of open-air recreation groups were of course part of people's multi-sensory and embodied engagements with those they were singing with, and the environments they sang within. For instance, writing about her experiences of a CHA holiday in 1933, Miss Phyllis Bell recounted a memorable 'day when we walked into a thunder-burst, and got soaked, but still went on walking and singing through the rain'.[12] As well as being a physical process with an audible sensory output, singing and sound can evoke emotional feeling, memories and imaginative connections.[13] It is impossible to disentangle singing completely from this complex, intersensorial engagement with the world; however, the focus of this Element will be to foreground and bring attention to the role of open-air singing, and how that both contributed to the sonic environments, or soundscapes, of rural and countryside places, highlighting

---

[8] Barbara Bender, 'Time and Landscape', *Current Anthropology*, 43: S4 (2002), s103–s112, p. S107. Christopher Tilley, *A Phenomenology of Landscape: Places, Paths and Monuments* (Oxford: Berg Publishers, 1994) p. 15.

[9] Tim Ingold and Jo Lee Vergunst, 'Introduction', in Tim Ingold and J. L., Vergunst (eds), *Ways of Walking: Ethnography and Practice on Foot* (Farnham: Ashgate, 2008) 1–20, p. 10.

[10] Christopher Tilley and Kate Cameron-Daum, *An Anthropology of Landscape: The Extraordinary in the Ordinary* (London: UCL Press, 2017), p. 7.

[11] Dara Culhane, 'Sensing', in Denielle Elliott and Dara Culhane (eds), *A Different Kind of Ethnography: Imaginative Practices and Creative Methodologies* (New York: University of Toronto Press, 2017), 45–68.

[12] Miss Phyllis Bell, 'Impressions of a First C.H.A. Holiday', *Comradeship: The Magazine of the Co-operative Holidays Association*, 25 (December 1933), 9–10, p. 9.

[13] Steven Feld, 'Waterfalls of Song: An Acoustemology of Place Resounding in Bosavi, Papua New Guinea', in Steven Feld and K. Basso (eds) *Senses of Place* (Santa Fe: School of American Research Press, 2011), 91–135, p. 97.

connections with other senses where appropriate.[14] We also argue that the sensory and the emotional are intertwined and cannot easily be separated. This follows Rob Boddice, who notes the senses are directly tied to a broader conceptual language of 'feeling'.[15] Similarly David Howes argues 'sensory studies plays up the double meaning of the term of "sense". This term encompasses both sensation and signification, feeling and meaning (as in the "sense" of a word) in its spectrum of referents'.[16] Our focus on sound and singing recognises that, within this embodied and multi-sensory, phenomenological perspective, sound is integral to how people experience, engage with and make sense of place.[17] We are, therefore, interested in the role of open-air singing in how people constructed, understood and even challenged conceptions of the English countryside.

Diverse forms of singing are a core part of human experience and their origins may stretch back over a million years. For instance, the value of group singing was recorded in Babylonia in the nineteenth century BCE.[18] It is a form of expression across human life cycles: from the lullabies sung to new-borns to the mourning songs of burial practices. Communal singing can share emotions and spirituality; it can create empathy, bolster identity and the boundaries of belonging, or challenge and protest social norms.[19] Open-air communal singing has been part of many spheres of human social life, including the traditional songs that find their origins in the rhythms of agricultural work and singing practices associated with team sports, such as football chants.[20]

Attention has been paid to the role of singing in relation to health, nature and emotions by social scientists as discussed by Sarah Bell, Clare Hickman and Frank Houghton in their survey on work relating to the concept of therapeutic sensescapes. They argue that although most research focuses on the sounds of nature or quiet spaces, there is work on the importance of music 'as well as a sense of connection experienced while singing in park and woodland settings'.[21] In the

---

[14] For more on soundscapes, see Raymond Murray Schafer, *The Soundscape: Our Sonic Environment and the Tuning of the World*, Rochester, Vermont: Destiny Books, 1994.
[15] Rob Boddice, *The History of Emotions* (Manchester: Manchester University Press, 2023), 151–152.
[16] David Howes, *The Sensory Studies Manifesto: Tracking the Sensorial Revolution in the Arts and Human Sciences* (Toronto: University of Toronto Press, 2022), 17.
[17] Feld, 'Waterfalls of Song', 91–135, p. 97.
[18] Esther M. Morgan-Ellis, and Kay Norton, 'Introduction: Singing as Community, Singing into Community, and Growing the Singing Community', in *The Oxford Handbook of Community Singing* (Oxford: Oxford University Press, 2024), pp. xxi–xxviii.
[19] John Potter and Neil Sorrell, *A History of Singing* (Cambridge: Cambridge University Press, 2012).
[20] Steve Roud, *Folk Song in England* (London: Faber and Faber, 2017); Pieter Schoonderwoerd, '"Shall We Sing a Song for You?": Mediation, Migration and Identity in Football Chants and Fandom', *Soccer & Society*, 12:1 (2010), 120–141. https://doi.org/10.1080/14560970.2011.530482.
[21] Sarah Bell, Clare Hickman and Frank Houghton, 'From Therapeutic Landscape to Therapeutic "Sensescape" Experiences with Nature? A Scoping Review', *Wellbeing, Space and Society*, 4 (2022), online: 1–11, p. 5.

case of one Belgian study a 'participant explained the sense of freedom of exteriorising emotions at the coast through screaming, crying and singing, gaining a sense of peace in the process'.[22] As Bell et al. noted quoting Duffy et al., 'this work suggests value in examining the role of sound in shaping "the euphoria of communicating back-and-forth between the self and others ... the sensation of becoming part of a collective – or one shared body" through more-than-human social and sonic landscape encounters'.[23]

Although very aware of the particular historical contingencies of our material, the use of historic as well as contemporary sources and voices will add to this literature on the emotional, therapeutic and sometimes exclusive rather than inclusive role of out-door singing. As Hedley Twidle and Aragorn Eloff argue, 'The ability of sound to pass through (and to behave differently in) different bodies, substrates, and environments makes it an intriguing and often surprising way to think through received categories and boundaries, whether "natural" or "cultural".'[24] We also recognise that these sonic experiences and expressions are highly contextual and dynamic: the 'phenomenal properties of sound are not fixed and universal; rather they are actively produced by the performative relations of making music'.[25]

Many of the emotional experiences described in our source material relate to community and fellowship through membership of a group. This sits within a wider literature where, as Katie Barclay has outlined, 'group cultures are also an important location for emotion, allowing people to form "refuges" of feeling within systems where they were excluded (such as in some gay subcultures), or giving shape to the dynamics of particular environments'.[26] Our focus on singing communities allows us to consider how emotions are shaped and experienced in relation to this shared physical sensory activity as well as the wider political, social and cultural pressures which also shape the group dynamics. As Mark Smith argues, there is a strong historical interrelationship between the development of social and sensory history.[27]

In terms of environmental history, as Peter Coates has outlined, 'at the risk of stating the obvious, all aural history is environmental in that it deals with sounds in physical settings, whether indoors or outdoors', which is a good starting point for

---

[22] *Ibid.* [23] *Ibid.*
[24] Hedley Twidle and Aragorn Elaff, 'Sounding Environments', in Emily O'Gorman, William San Martín, Mark Carey and Sandra Swart (eds), *The Routledge Handbook of Environmental History* (1st ed.) (London: Routledge, 2023), 49–65, p. 51.
[25] George Revill, 'Music and the Politics of Sound: Nationalism, Citizenship, and Auditory Space', *Environment and Planning D: Society and Space*, 18: 5 (2000), 597–613, p. 598.
[26] Kate Barclay, 'State of the Field: The History of Emotions', *History*, 106 (2021), 456–466.
[27] Mark M. Smith, *The Sensory Manifesto* (University Park: Penn State University Press, 2021).

our foray into the intersections of bodies, communities, places and other species as experienced through outdoor singing.[28] Attending to sound in environmental history not only 'invites us to listen across time' but to also attend to the entanglement of human and other-than-human elements of soundscapes.[29] Victoria Bates has noted that '"soundscape" remains a useful shorthand. It refers simultaneously to the different sounds that – when perceived, through feeling and/or hearing – make up the profile of a given space or place, and it brings together the material and social aspects of sound'.[30] However, as Gaynor et al. note, environmental historians are only recently making 'emotion a central category of analysis'.[31] We, therefore, hope to add to the growing body of work discussing the role of emotions, as well as the senses, in relation to human–environment interactions.

In this Element we focus on three key areas to consider the sensory and emotional histories of open-air singing in the early twentieth century. The first places the bodily experience at the centre of the discussion and examines the various ways in which the body relates to the environment, primarily via the air as well as to others through the physical act of singing. The second explores the creation of fellow feeling through song and its ability to both include and exclude others as well as develop relationships beyond the human. The third key section focuses on the sensory and emotional relationships to place that are both created and memorialised via song as well as the role that sound and singing play in contested ways of being in the countryside that this examination reveals. Finally, we consider the contemporary connections and resonances through the former three themes to move beyond the archival historical research to ask what the experience of singing groups today can tell us about relationships to their bodies, other beings and places. Our conclusion looks forward and asks what future research might achieve by taking these approaches to considering the role of outdoor song in both the past and present.

1 Sensing and Feeling the Landscape via the Body

The exercise of Synging is delightful to Nature and good to preserve ye Health of Man. It doth strengthen all parts of ye brest and doth open ye pipes.
                                                                    –Byrd, 1588.[32]

---

[28] Peter A. Coates, 'The Strange Stillness of the Past: Toward an Environmental History of Sound and Noise', *Environmental History*, 10: 4 (2005), 636–65, p. 638.
[29] Twidle and Elaff, 'Sounding Environments'.
[30] Victoria Bates, *Making Noise in the Modern Hospital*, Series: Elements in Histories of Emotions and the Senses (Cambridge: Cambridge University Press, 2021), p. 9.
[31] Andrea Gaynor, Susan Broomhall and Andy Flack, 'Frogs and Feeling Communities: A Study in History of Emotions and Environmental History', *Environment and History*, 28 (2022), 83–104.
[32] As quoted in the foreword of The Holiday Fellowship, *Songs by the Way* (no date of publication is given but it was likely published in the 1920s).

The foreword of the song book *Songs by the Way*, produced by and for members of the HF in the 1920s, opens with the quote above by the composer William Byrd. Taken from two statements in 1588 published within Byrd's own songbook, *Psalmes, sonets, & songs of sadnes and pietie*, as part of a list of 'Reasons briefely set downe by th' author to perswade everyone to learne to sing'.[33] This not only demonstrates the long history of singing as a practice understood in connection to physical health and breath but also the ways in which twentieth-century organisations, such as the HF, were positioning their own practice of singing in relation to Byrd's argument.

The use of this approach in the 1920s is particularly interesting as the first decades of the century saw a renewed interest in 'natural' open-air exercises for health including 'games, swimming, field sports, and dancing', which were promoted by many medical practitioners including the then Chief Medical Officer, Sir George Newman.[34] For organisations like the HF and various rambling and holiday societies, this also included the joint activities of walking and singing. In many ways this emerged out of late nineteenth-century Christian muscularity which encouraged the development of a strong healthy body through sport, as well as a growing sense of bodily health related to breath and song expressed by some medical practitioners.[35] This section aims to place the physicality of the singing body at the centre of the discussion and to consider how conceptions of air, breath, song and movement were connected to each other as well as the surrounding environment.

1.1 Air and the Body

As the scholars Tatiana Konrad, Chantelle Mitchell and Savannah Schaufler have recently written, 'air is a consistent biological necessity, indispensable to human and more-than-human beings, to life and survival', as well as something that at the same time is 'materially and ideologically complex; at once an environmental and scientific concern, . . ., and register of entanglement, relation, and well-being'.[36] It is therefore both simple in its indispensability and complicated in its relationality to the environment and other living beings. The

---

[33] William Byrd, *Psalmes, Sonets, & Songs [...]* (London, 1599). ProQuest. [Accessed 31 January 2025]. https://www.proquest.com/books/psalmes-sonets-songs-sadnes-pietie-made-into/docview/2240852014/se-2 (accessed November 20, 2025).

[34] Ina Zweiniger-Bargielowska, *Managing the Body: Beauty, Health, and Fitness in Britain, 1880–1939* (Oxford: Oxford University Press, 2010), p. 157.

[35] Jennifer Sheppard, 'Sound of Body: Music, Sports and Health in Victorian Britain', *Journal of the Royal Musical Association*, 140: 2 (2015), 343–369.

[36] Tatiana Konrad, Chantelle Mitchell and Savannah Schaufler, 'Introduction: Toward a Cultural Axiology of Air', in Tatiana Konrad (ed) *Imagining Air: Cultural Axiology and the Politics of Invisibility* (Exeter: University of Exeter Press, 2023) 1–34, p. 1.

first and last breaths we take are the key moments marking the beginning and the end of life – it punctuates everything. As Konrad et al. write, 'breath as a bodily function, in which each inhalation registers direct contact with the external world, sees the alveoli, pleural cavity, the branches of the lungs, as sites of exchange – with air at once both inside and outside'.[37] The body is made permeable through many mechanisms, but the rhythmical process of breathing is a key method by which we are all physically connected to our environment.

Air, however, has not always been conceptualised as one single element and it has existed in multiple contexts. For example, the ancient Greek Hippocratic tradition distinguished between different types of air: there was external air (*aer, eeros*) and external wind (*pneuma, anemos*), as well as inner wind or breath (*pneuma, physa*).[38] The importance of the relationship between the environment and the body in early medicine is even captured in the title of one of the key Hippocratic works, *Airs, Waters, Places*. Although, by 1733, at a time of great interest in the physical properties of air, the physician John Arbuthnot could complain that physicians, unlike Philosophers, Mathematicians, Chemists and 'Professors of Agriculture and Garden', had not paid enough attention to the effects of air on the body.[39] The reason for this lack of interest he suggested was that 'air is of those *Ingesta*, or things taken inwardly, which neither can be forborn nor measur'd in Doses'.[40] This highlights the historical complexities of something which is essential for life, is everywhere and is therefore taken for granted and yet cannot be easily controlled in terms of how much crosses the boundaries of our bodies. As Christopher Sellers, has argued 'both environmental and medical historians can seek to understand the past two centuries of medical history in terms of a seesaw dialogue over the ways and means by which physicians and other health professionals did, and also did not, consider the influence of place – airs and waters included – on disease'.[41] Given our focus on modern Britain we will limit ourselves here to noting just these examples from the Western medical tradition, but we recognise that other cultures and times have also had their own conceptions and

---

[37] *Ibid.*, p. 2.
[38] Eugenio Frixione, 'Pneuma–Fire Interactions in Hippocratic Physiology', *Journal of the History of Medicine and Allied Sciences*, 68: 4 (2013), 505–528.
[39] John Arbuthnot, *An Essay Concerning the Effects of Air on Human Bodies* (Printed for J. Tonson in the Strand, 1733), p. vi. Eighteenth Century Collections Online, link.gale.com/apps/doc/CW0107175801/ECCO?u=new_itw&sid=bookmark-ECCO&xid=9e432cc5&pg=4. [Accessed 31 January 2025].
[40] *Ibid.*
[41] Christopher Sellers, 'To Place or Not to Place: Toward an Environmental History of Modern Medicine', *Bulletin of the History of Medicine*, 92: 1 (2018), 1–45.

understandings of the relationship of air and the body in terms of health given its centrality to life.

Breath, speech and song are all interconnected physiological processes, as at the most basic level they all involve the inhalation and expulsion of air via the lungs. The main difference between them being whether conscious sound is made through this process, and, if it is, what kind of sound is produced. As Gillian Kayes explains, 'breathing and phonation [vibration initiated by the vocal folds] are closely linked in vocal function: in singing and speech production the sound source can be "voiced" – a result of vocal fold vibration – or "unvoiced" – a result of air passing through a constriction above the vocal folds'.[42] The physicality of singing with its focus on a particularly high physiological use of air in comparison to general breathing emphasises this bodily connection with the external environment and is often viewed as a process by which health can be improved or restored.

As contemporary voice scholars Jing Kang, Austin Scholp and Jack Jiang note, 'recent years have witnessed an incremental recognition of the value of singing activities in improving mental and physical health in both nonclinical and clinical settings'.[43] Although they also recognise that these are not new ideas and trace these origins back to the early twentieth century, stating that 'as early as 1930, Rollrath found that many famous singers had lived to be 80 or even more than 100 years old, which suggested that singing could increase longevity'.[44] As we have seen above Byrd was already making connections about improving physical health by singing in the sixteenth century, but the idea of tying the physical act of singing to health and longevity fits within a wider narrative found in this early twentieth-century period of the role of air in relation to both exercise and, as we will explore here, singing outdoors. Potential reasons for longevity worth noting were not only confined to the practice of singing – the air itself was considered a factor. For example, in the 1959–60 SCR handbook numerous instances of longevity in Derbyshire were linked specifically to the air itself.[45] Although the type of quality of the Derbyshire air is not specified in this piece, we can safely assume that what is implied is rural or country air rather than that which is found in urban settings.

Ideas concerning health and rural leisure activities in the early twentieth-century were part of a cosmology of understanding where urban conditions

---

[42] Gillyanne Kayes, 'Structure and Function of the Singing Voice', in Graham F. Welch, David M. Howard and John Nix (eds), *The Oxford Handbook of Singing*, Oxford Library of Psychology (2019; online ed., Oxford Academic) 3–30, p. 3.

[43] Jing Kang, Austin Scholp and Jack J. Jiang, 'A Review of the Physiological Effects and Mechanisms of Singing', *Journal of Voice*, 32: 4 (2018), 390–395, p. 390.

[44] *Ibid.*

[45] Anon, 'It's the Derbyshire Air', *Sheffield Clarion Ramblers Handbook 1959–60*, p. 78.

were deemed unhealthy in contrast to the widely imagined countryside as a source of health and wellbeing. This reflects what Bill Luckin and Keir Waddington have described as the pro-rural/anti-urban sentiment that emerged in the nineteenth century and was strengthened by the concerns around physical and mental degeneration of the population at the end of the nineteenth century.[46] One widespread concern related in particular to the high rates of Tuberculosis (TB) which reached their height in Europe towards the middle of the century. It is thought that in 1850 tuberculosis was responsible for one in four deaths worldwide and, according to Richard Morris, 'until the 1870s it was the number one killer of Britons'.[47]

As TB predominately affects the lungs, one central medical concept which emerged was that time spent in the 'open-air' (preferably rural or coastal outdoor air) should be viewed as an essential preventative and therapeutic approach for dealing with this and other related diseases. There were variations on what this meant in practice, but generally this led to patients spending as much time as possible in outdoor settings, even tents and wooden chalets, to obtain the maximum amounts of fresh air and sunshine. This became intertwined with ideas about healthy outdoor recreation and access for urban dwellers to more rural spaces.[48] As E. A. Letts argued in his 1892 lecture, *The Air We Breathe*: 'we live *in* air, and to a certain extent *on* air, for it is continually flowing into our blood. No wonder, then, that we are influenced by climate, which means the condition of the air'.[49] This is echoed in recent work on air which conceptualises it as the '*medium* and breathing the *mechanism* through which the outside environment is embodied. Air carries the weather, climate and particles from the environment into the body. Humans embody the climate of their environment through air, just as fish embody the climate of their environment through water'.[50]

---

[46] Bill Luckin, *Death and Survival in Urban Britain: Disease, Pollution and Environment, 1800–1950* (London: Bloomsbury, 2015); Keir Waddington, '"In a Country Every Way by Nature Favourable to Health": Landscape and Public Health in Victorian Rural Wales', *Canadian Bulletin of Medical History*, 31: 2 (2014), 183–204.

[47] Richard E. Morris, 'The Victorian "Change of Air" as Medical and Social Construction', *Journal of Tourism History*, 10: 1 (2018), 49–65, p. 51.

[48] Clare Hickman, 'The Importance of Open Air for Health: Environmental and Medical Intersections', in Tatiana Konrad (ed) *Imagining Air: Cultural Axiology and the Politics of Invisibility* (Exeter: University of Exeter Press, 2023), 180–199.

[49] Edmund A. Letts, 'The Air We Breathe', in *The body and Its Health: Being a Course of Lectures Delivered under the Auspices of the Belfast Society for the Extension of University Teaching* (Belfast: Olley, 1892), 67–96. Wellcome Collection. https://wellcomecollection.org/works/v56emh5k.

[50] Megan Wainwright, 'Sensing the Airs: The Cultural Context for Breathing and Breathlessness in Uruguay', *Medical Anthropology*, 36: 4 (2017), 332–347, pp. 342–343.

Similarly, in his introduction to the book *How to Conquer Consumption* (consumption was another term commonly used for TB), published in 1926, David Masters emphasised these interrelated concerns about air, environment and the body, writing:

> People who had been used to working in the open air were imprisoned all day in dusty factories, and whether they were inside or outside, waking or sleeping, the air they breathed was always laden with the impurities that are inseparable from the atmosphere of an industrial centre where factory chimneys and blast furnaces so foul the heavens with fumes and atoms of carbon that all vegetation is stunted within their areas. . . . The newcomers to industry were denied that breath of pure fresh air which cleansed their lungs and re-oxygenated their blood so long as they lived in the country.[51]

There is a sense of nostalgia in all these pieces for a time before industrialisation and urbanisation when people were more commonly employed as agrarian workers in rural communities. Dr David Chowry Muthu, an Indian physician who established the Mendip Hills Sanatorium in the UK and the Tambaram Sanatorium in India thought a solution to the health issues facing the nation could be found if the Poor Law was abolished and the poor were given free access to the land. He argued that these measures would mean:

> more employment in the country, more honourable work done under health-giving conditions ... It would mean pure and wholesome occupation to thousands of citizens living in the open air and pleasant sunshine, and engaged in the congenial task of tilling the fields and gathering in the harvest ... It would mean that in many a cottage home the family altar would be set up, and a 'race of pure heart, iron sinew, splendid frame, and constant faith', would keep alive the bygone traditions of its yeoman fathers.[52]

He brought these ideas into his practice by recommending that TB patients that were recovering well should go 'tramping' in the countryside (see Figure 2), arguing:

> What a change this tramping life would bring to the town-bred patient. The rosy flush of the early dawn, the morning chant of the birds, the sunlit fields and meadows fill him with new delights; while the afterglow of the sunset, the hush of the twilight, the radiance of the starlit sky calm his mind and still his soul into quietness and peace. And as he lies down to rest he nestles close to the bosom of mother Nature and lets her wrap him in dreamless sleep.[53]

---

[51] David Masters, *How to Conquer Consumption* (London: John Lane, Bodley Head, 1926), p. 189.
[52] David Chowry Muthu, *Pulmonary Tuberculosis and Sanatorium Treatment: A Record of 10 years' Observation and Work in Open-Air Sanatoria* (London: Balliere, Tindall and Cox, 1910), pp. 192–193.
[53] David Chowry Muthu, *Pulmonary Tuberculosis: Its Etiology and Treatment. A Record of Twenty Two Years' Observation and Work in Open-Air Sanatoria* (London: Balliere, Tindall and Cox, 1922), p. 246.

Figure 2 Photograph of three patients (two women and one man) in Edwardian dress on a tramping tour or long walk in the countryside.
From David Chowry Muthu, *Pulmonary Tuberculosis: Its Etiology and Treatment. A Record of Twenty Two Years' Observation and Work in Open-Air Sanatoria* (London: Balliere, Tindall and Cox, 1922). Credit: Wellcome Collection.

Muthu, like many physicians treating conditions such as TB at this time, viewed open-air therapies as the answer (as a preventative as well as a therapeutic measure) and argued in 1910 that 'the secret of its widespread interest in Europe is due to the discovery – if discovery it may be called – that fresh air, hitherto regarded as an enemy to be shut out and barred, is really a friend, and one of Nature's best gifts to man'.[54] Others such as the retired Lieutenant, J. P. Muller (previously of the Danish Army), who wrote the book, *My Sun-Bathing and Fresh-Air System*, also saw this natural method for health as a way to manage the issues brought on by modern life. He argued, 'Man is subject to more bodily ills to-day than he has ever been before, and it is only natural, when you come to consider it, that the descendants of a race who had to hunt their food before they could eat should not be able to work in a factory or an office without

---

[54] Muthu, *Pulmonary Tuberculosis and Sanatorium Treatment*, pp. 83–84.

suffering for it in some way or another.'[55] These pro-rural/anti-urban nostalgic themes were also at the heart of late nineteenth-century and early twentieth-century movements, including the Arts and Crafts and Garden City Movements.[56]

These ideas are also picked up in G. H. B. Ward's 1922, foreword to the SCR's songbook, *Songs for Ramblers to Sing on the Moorlands*, where he describes how traditional songs are particularly appropriate for singing outdoors because of their inherent connectedness and resonance with not just the landscape but the open-air itself. Ward writes: 'what better medium could we desire than the old English country folk song with its simple appeal and the very breath of the countryside in its jingling rhymes'.[57] This nostalgia for the simplicity of the past as well as the concerns around air and health are brought together in the description of the air as 'the very breath of the countryside'.[58] Similarly, the founding ethos of the CHA was in part around the health benefits of rambling and being in the rural open air. Occasionally this made it into the choice of songs by outdoor recreation groups. For instance, the lyrics of 'On Trek!' (the marching song of the scouts) include the line 'Boys, we are going where the clean winds blow!'[59] Another example published in the SCR songbook 'A mountain thought' contains the line 'The health-born winds about us whirl', and the line 'With a heigh-ho! In the fresh air' is a repeated refrain in the rewrite of 'Come to the fair', titled 'A dinner table song'.[60]

Rural walking was itself encouraged as a healthy practice because of its action on the lungs (see Figure 3). In 1908, an article in *The Circle* magazine (which was aimed at children within the co-operative movement) titled 'Pleasures of the Countryside' extolled the physical virtues of walking in the countryside. The author argued that 'walking is the most healthful form of exercise, because it brings practically all the muscles of the body into action, while the lungs are refreshed and strengthened by breathing the pure air'.[61] Along with a discussion of the importance of natural history knowledge and observation, it is clear that getting outside was encouraged for the health of children as well as adults. A short piece entitled 'On Walking' in the 1959–60 SCR handbook described how one could not 'help but feel pity for the townsmen' who experienced 'No pleasure in walking, that strengthens the limbs and invigorates the lungs!'[62]

---

[55] Jørgen Peter Muller, *My Sun-Bathing and Fresh-Air System* (London: Athletic, 1927), p. 17.
[56] See Clare Hickman, *Therapeutic Landscapes: A History of English Hospital Gardens since 1800* (Manchester: Manchester University Press, 2013), pp. 157–158.
[57] Ward, *Songs for Ramblers to Sing on the Moorlands*, p. 1.   [58] Ibid.
[59] Arthur Poyser (ed), *The Open Air Songbook* (London: The Boy Scouts Association, 1947), p. 203.
[60] Ward, *Songs for Ramblers to Sing on the Moorlands*, p. 4, p. 11.
[61] Anon, 'Pleasures of the Countryside', *The Circle*, 1: 9 (1908), p. 217.
[62] E. C., 'On Walking', *Sheffield Clarion Ramblers Handbook 1959–60*, p. 76.

Figure 3 'Come Rambling': a 1950s poster for The Ramblers' Association depicting a young (and implicitly healthy) couple walking in a rural landscape. Credit: Image courtesy of The Ramblers.

Edward Carpenter, a leading cultural, political and social reformer, was one of those heavily involved in the wider movement to encourage outside recreation. As Ina Zweiniger-Bargielowska has discussed in detail, Carpenter delivered a lecture to the Fabian Society titled, *Civilization, Its Cause and Cure* in 1889, in which he claimed that civilisation was a 'disease' that was 'physical, social, intellectual, and moral'.[63] He contrasted this by looking at the '"higher types of savages" whose "superabundant health" was due to regular "shouting, singing, dancing", and a culture in harmony with nature'.[64] As Zweiniger-Bargielowska argues, in Carpenter's view 'health was more than a "purely negative" absence of disease. It could only be acquired by the "adoption

---

[63] Zweiniger-Bargielowska, *Managing the Body*, p. 27. [64] *Ibid.*

of a healthy life, bodily and mental'".[65] This involved a '"return to nature", a "life of the open air", "clean and pure food", and "companionship of the animals'".[66] Along with the open air, he recommended sunlight and sunbaths which were also central elements of the sanatoria regimen and chime with the health practices of both Muthu and Muller as discussed above. We have a sense then that Carpenter considered that perfect health could be achieved through physical activities out-doors, 'in harmony with nature', including singing which takes us back to Byrd's quote about singing as 'delightful to nature'. It is also worth noting here that the founder of the SCR, G. H. B Ward, considered Carpenter a friend and mentor, and quoted his writing numerous times within the pages of the club's annual handbooks. As such, we can see that Carpenter's ideas influenced both the practices and ethos of the club.

Carpenter was far from being alone in his belief in the power of singing. In 1901 a US physician, S. A. Knopf, outlined how

> Barth, of Köslin, who has made a careful study of the effects of singing on the action of the lungs and heart ..., has come to the conclusion that singing is one of the exercises most conducive to health. Considering the fact that it can be practiced anywhere (when the air is pure) or at any time, without apparatus, it should be much more cultivated than it actually is.[67]

Similarly, Muthu recommended singing exercises as an ideal way for TB sufferers to recover their strength arguing that 'they invoke correct nasal breathing, maintain a better expansion of the chest and a freer passage of air to remote parts of the lung, such as the apices – which are liable to become tuberculous owing to their comparative inactivity – and determine a more efficient supply of blood to these parts, and thus indirectly improve the local and general health'.[68] He even included breathing and singing exercises at 10.00 am every day in the example given in his book of the daily programme for patients at his sanatorium.[69] The body was understood to need access to clean, fresh air to fulfil its healthy potential and singing was an easy way to maximise the strength of the lungs and the volume of air inhaled.

Alongside this there were also perceived moral benefits of a closer relationship to nature as both breathing and singing were methods by which the human/environment barrier was constantly breached. As Konrad writes, 'despite its

---

[65] *Ibid.* [66] *Ibid.*
[67] Sigard A. Knopf, 'Respiratory Exercises in the Prevention and Treatment of Pulmonary Diseases', *Johns Hopkins Medical Bulletin*, 12: 126 (1901), 282–288. This article is also later quoted in Guy Hinsdale, *Atmospheric Air in Relation to Tuberculosis* (Washington, DC: Smithsonian Institute, 1914) p. 102, which suggests that there was a long-lasting interest in the topic.
[68] Muthu, *Pulmonary Tuberculosis: Its Etiology and Treatment*, p. 243 [69] *Ibid.*, p. 229.

alleged invisibility and imperceptibility, air is an essential part of the larger environment in which humans exist'.[70] Ingold similarly argues against seeing the material aspects of the world as mainly landscape and artefacts without the inclusion of air.[71] Materiality according to him is not just an expression of entanglements between people and 'things' but between people and mediums like air and water. This interrelationship between bodies, air and the environment is highlighted in the SCR song 'An after dinner ditty', where one of the lines describes how 'As they strolled across the moorland, on the air their voices rang'.[72] Here the bodies are moving and physically interacting with the environment in several different ways or as Ingold states, 'a living, breathing body is at once a body-on-the-ground and a body-in-the-air'.[73]

On top of these basic tenets of bodies moving and breathing, we can also layer the changeability and vulnerability of the body to the environment which is perhaps highlighted most through accounts of the sensory experience of weather. As Ingold writes 'we hear these textures in the rain from the sounds of drops falling on diverse materials, and we touch and smell in the keen wind that – piercing the body – opens it up and sharpens its haptic and olfactory responses'.[74] Although, as Howes has noted, 'the body' is not a singular thing; there are individual differences in the way bodies sense due to gender, race and class, and that multisensory perception is complex and nuanced.[75] The air itself also has material qualities but so do other aspects of weather like rain and snow. Singing in our research is clearly also used to manage the bodily and emotional challenges created by the weather. For example, in 1926 Stephen Graham described how when walking in the rain 'after five of ten miles one begins to sing', ensuring one completes the walk 'in the highest of spirits' despite being wet through.[76] In this way, singing is a form of motivation and emotional self-regulation in the context of embodied experiences of exertion and weather.

1.2 Resonations

Resonations can be both vibrations that are physically felt in the body or heard in the environment as well as metaphorical and symbolic. Writing about sonic

---

[70] Tatiana Konrad (ed) *Race and Environmental Justice in the Era of Climate Change and COVID-19*, (Michigan: Michigan State University Press, 2025), p. 5.
[71] Tim Ingold, 'Footprints through the Weather-World: Walking, Breathing, Knowing', *Journal of the Royal Anthropological Institute*, 16: 1 (2010), 121–139, p.S130.
[72] Ward, *Songs for Ramblers to Sing on the Moorlands*, p. 15.
[73] Ingold, 'Footprints through the Weather-World', p. S122.   [74] *Ibid.*, p. S131.
[75] David Howes, 'The Misperception of the Environment: A Critical Evaluation of the Work of Tim Ingold and an Alternative Guide to the Use of the Senses in Anthropological Theory', *Anthropological Theory*, 22: 4 (2022), 443–466, p. 450.
[76] Stephen Graham, *The Gentle Art of Tramping* (New York: D. Appleton, 1926), p. 147.

resonances in the context of environmental history, Twidle and Elaff highlight sound as both a noun and verb; 'both physical property (a sound) and open-ended process (to sound or sound out, to enquire into or investigate)'.[77] In terms of a physical property, Michael Benninger writes that 'for any instrument to produce sound, something must activate the sound (such as plucking a string on a guitar or blowing into a trumpet), something must vibrate (like the guitar string or the reed), and something must resonate (the body of the instrument)'.[78] This singular act of the body resonated can have a wide-reaching affect. According to George Revill, 'the physical properties of sound, pitch, rhythm, timbre seem to act on and through the body in ways which require neither explanation nor reflection. This appears to grant music a singular power to play on the emotions, to arouse and subdue, animate and pacify'.[79] In its most simple terms when singing the body is the instrument and the resonations come from the exhalation of air via the chest and the head. The environment via the air can then be said to physically resonate within the body as well as outside of it or as Michael Stocker states 'our sense of sound includes the embrace of our body by the environment'.[80]

In this Element we focus on group singing and there has been some recent scholarly research pointing to the particular health benefits of this activity. Although we cannot apply this directly to the past, it is worth considering the ways in which we currently understand these mechanisms to work in relation to both the physical body and the mind. For example, David Camlin, Helena Daffern and Katherine Zeserson have published research on the wellbeing effects of outdoor group singing on participants of three groups. From this they argue that one key element that makes group singing effective is the 'phenomenon of interpersonal "resonance"' as the basis of the shared experience, which, they argue 'explains why it might contribute positively to the experience not just of social bonding, but also the underlying neurobiological mechanism of the experience of "love"'.[81] They quote Siegle's explanation for this phenomenon that 'when we attune to others we allow our own internal state

---

[77] Twidle and Elaff, 'Sounding Environments', p. 52.
[78] Michael S. Benninger and Jean Abitbol, 'Voice: Dysphonia and the Ageing Voice in American Academy of Otolaryngology - Head and Neck Surgery Foundation', *Geriatric Care Otolaryngology* (Alexandria, VA: American Academy of Otolaryngology - Head and Neck Surgery Foundation, 2006), 67–81. https://rlmc.edu.pk/themes/images/gallery/library/books/ENT/Geriatric%20Care%20Otolaryngology.pdf.
[79] Revill, 'Music and the Politics of Sound: Nationalism, Citizenship, and Auditory Space', p. 602.
[80] Michael Stocker, *Hear Where We Are: Sound, Ecology and Sense of Place* (New York: Springer, 2013), p. 3.
[81] David Camlin, Helena Daffern and Katherine Zeserson, 'Group Singing as a Resource for the Development of a Healthy Public', *Humanities and Social Science Communications* 7: 60 (2020), 1–15, p. 3.

to shift, to come to resonate with the inner world of another. This resonance is at the heart of the important sense of "feeling felt" that emerges in close relationships'.[82] From this they posit that wellbeing might not just be from the group participation element or the singing itself but rather that the production of musical effects reinforces 'interpersonal attunement and consequent individual wellbeing, a mutually reinforcing and complex adaptive process'.[83] As noted this is a contemporary study but there are clearly descriptions of 'fellow feeling' which are reinforced through group singing within our historic examples and these will be explored more in Section 2.

It is also possible to consider in this context that broader resonances with nature and other species, as well as other people might further reinforce this process, particularly as one of the participants within Camlin et al.'s project stated that 'somehow it was the mountains that were reverberating with us, if you see what I mean, rather than an audience'.[84] The experience of the sound here is inclusive of the mountains which are viewed as an active participant. As the researchers note, 'from the point of view of the participants, the way in which they come to feel a resonant connection with other individuals, with the group as a whole, with the music they are singing and its meaning, and their surroundings, appears to lie at the heart of what they feel is most powerful about the group singing experience'.[85]

In another example, Theorell has described how participants of choral groups self-report increased experience of joy and relaxation from singing together, as well as a sense of connection and cohesion with other choir members.[86] Other studies measured levels of oxytocin (a hormone thought to have a role in social-bonding) before and after activities and found higher oxytocin levels after group singing compared with simply chatting together. The factors affecting feelings of social and physical wellbeing from singing are complex, and Theorell concluded that the current state of evidence on the health benefits of group singing was modest and often indirect.[87] Another synthesis by Kang, Scholp and Jiang, citing Pearce et al., indicated it may be the extent to which participants felt integrated within their group, rather than the nature of the activity itself, that engenders perceived benefits.[88] However, they also cited research by Stewart and Lonsdale that suggested 'choral activities seemed to enhance the sense of belonging of the participants, co-ordinated within the singing itself to

---

[82] *Ibid.*, quoting Dan Siegel, *Mindsight: Transform Your Brain with the New Science of Kindness* (London: Oneworld, 2011), p. 27.
[83] *Ibid.*, p. 3. [84] *Ibid.*, p. 10. [85] *Ibid.*, p. 12.
[86] Töres Theorell, *Psychological Health Effects of Musical Experiences Theories, Studies and Reflections in Music Health Science* (SpringerBriefs in Psychology, 2014), pp. 17–27.
[87] *Ibid*, p. 84.
[88] Kang et al., 'A Review of the Physiological Effects and Mechanisms of Singing', p. 393.

further improve the well-being and quality of life'.[89] It should be noted that these synthesis articles mainly looked at group singing by formal choirs in indoor contexts. An exception is the Camlin et al. study which explored and compared the experiences of amateur adult group singers in both open-air and indoor settings. They found that 'while group singing may contribute to individual health and wellbeing, the primary benefit participants across both groups identified is the way that it brings them to a closer, more profound, connection with others'.[90] As these are contemporary examples they cannot be simply mapped onto the past but they do suggest that a healthful singing body can be achieved within a group in specific ways, which relate to resonances with others whether they are human, animal or part of the wider place or environment.

One aspect that is potentially less relevant for today's singing groups, although not for all, is the role of the divine as a key element within the environment. The founder of the CHA and HF, T. A. Leonard, began his career as a congregational church pastor before deciding to 'devote the whole of his energy and ability to the holiday movement' which highlights how close these connections could be.[91] The first song in *Songs by the Way* published by the HF was 'The Strength of the Hills' by Mrs Hemans and includes this verse which depicts God within the air and other natural phenomena:

> For the dark resounding mountains
> Where Thy still small voice is heard,
> For the strong pines in the forest,
> Which by Thy breath are stirred;
> For the storm on whose free pinions
> Thy Spirit walks abroad,
> For the strength of the hills we bless Thee,
> Our God, our fathers' God.[92]

Here God is present within the mountains and forests and is the creator of air via his breath, so singing outdoors would have an added layer of emotional and spiritual resonance beyond that of the physical realm.

1.3 Emotions and Senses of Wellbeing

The interrelationships between singing, emotions and wellbeing have already been touched on in relation to group singing practices. However, the physicality

---

[89] *Ibid.*
[90] Camlin et al., 'Group Singing as a Resource for the Development of a Healthy Public', p. 8.
[91] N. H. Gregory, 'T.A. Leonard: The Pioneer of Fellowship Holidays', *Millgate Monthly* 36, Part 2: 311 (August 1931), 643–647, p. 644.
[92] The Holiday Fellowship, *Fellowship Holidays: Programme & Songs* (The Holiday Fellowship, 1929) p. 3.

of singing is clearly an important feature when considering senses of wellbeing. For example, as Feld argues there is a 'special bodily nexus for sensation and emotion' when sound, hearing and voice are brought together due to 'their coordination of brain, nervous system, head, ear, chest, muscles, respiration, and breathing'.[93] In the case of outdoor walking, movement is also brought into play as our groups were often walking and hiking together as well as singing.

In a 1926 chapter on 'Marching Songs', Graham reflects on the interplay between rambling and singing:

> Yet singing is very natural, and when one takes to the road the singing impulse comes to the bosom. Light-heartedness begets song. We sing as we walk, we walk as we sing, and the kilometers fall behind. After a long spell of the forced habit of not singing one finds oneself accidentally singing, and there is surprise. Good Heavens! I'm singing.[94]

Although the regular beat of a marching song may help maintain pace and rhythm when walking, Arthur Sidgwick in 1912 posited that stronger drivers for the connection of walking and singing were the links to 'the actual bodily condition of a walker, that perfect harmony which comes of a frame well occupied' and the emotions engendered through rambling: 'It is on the mood which walking induces, rather than on the rhythmical character itself, that the affinity between walking and music mainly rests.'[95]

On an SCR rambling trip to Ambleside in 1919 the description of singing of *Come to the fair* at an evening concert articulates the close association between air, breath and emotions, and highlights the additional meaning of air as describing a melody: 'a lilting air, breathing the spirit of the week'.[96] A 'love of jollity' was a characteristic of the early SCR: 'Here boisterous good humour and kindly "divvlement" had free scope, and many a weary business man and toiler has temporarily forgotten his burden of care and gloom in the joyous revelry of our open air life.'[97]

In all of these accounts song is described as forming an important method by which the body moves and the mind responds to the external environment. As has been touched above and will be explored more fully in the next sections, it is also a way to build connections with other people, animals and places.

---

[93] Feld, 'Waterfalls of Song', p. 97.
[94] Graham, *The Gentle Art of Tramping*, p. 129.
[95] Arthur H. Sidgwick, *Walking Essays* (London: Edward Arnold, 1922), p. 68, pp. 80–81.
[96] Anon, 'The 1919 Whitsuntide (Climbing) Week, – Ambleside Lake District', *Sheffield Clarion Ramblers Handbook 1920–21*, 97–100, p. 100.
[97] The Wee Mon, 'Our Coming of Age Ramble, September 4th 1921', *Sheffield Clarion Ramblers Handbook 2022–23*, 56–60, p. 57.

2 Fellow-Feeling through Song

> *The object is to encourage the growth of the true open-air spirit of fellowship and love.*[98]

This quote from the foreword to the SCR songbook, *Songs for Ramblers to Sing on the Moorlands*, illustrates how communal singing was framed by early twentieth century open-air groups as a deliberately relational activity. Through collective, open-air singing people developed a sense of connection and fellow-feeling with both one another and with nature. This use of the word fellow-feeling is chosen by us to mean more than the term 'Fellowship' as used by the various organisations we are discussing. As Rob Boddice and Mark Smith argue 'historical concepts of experience often bear little resemblance to "emotion" or "sense", but rather combine affective and cognitive categories in more general concepts of feeling'.[99] Fellow-feeling in relation to our historical actors incorporates more than other humans as well as other concepts, such as potential civilising influences for the modern man and woman, something that will be expanded upon later. However, two concepts are worth noting as useful for our framing of understanding fellow-feeling: the historian Barbara Rosenwein's definition of emotional communities as groups 'that have their own particular values, modes of feeling, and ways to express those feelings,' and the anthropologists Victor and Edith Turner's notion of communitas as 'inspired fellowship'.[100] For Rosenwein, emotional communities are not always centred on emotions but 'share important norms concerning the emotions that they value and deplore and the modes of expressing them'.[101] Although tricky to pin down to a simple definition, Edith Turner has described communitas as a form of collective joy: 'a group's pleasure in sharing common experiences with one's fellows' and 'the sense felt by a plurality of people without boundaries'.[102] Communitas comes alive in many diverse settings, and the combination of shared activities such as singing, rambling, eating, drinking, learning, and holidaying together amongst outdoor recreation groups in the early twentieth century may have been fertile ground to inspire this.

In this section we interrogate the archival material to explore relationships between open-air singing and a feeling of community and fellowship. In particular, we consider how building fellow-feeling was one aim of early

---

[98] Ward, *Songs for Ramblers to Sing on the Moorlands*, p. 1.
[99] Rob Boddice and Mark Smith, *Emotion, Sense, Experience* (Cambridge: Cambridge University Press, 2020), p. 10.
[100] Barbara H. Rosenwein, *Generations of Feeling: A History of Emotions, 600–1700* (Cambridge: Cambridge University Press, 2015), p. 3; Edith Turner, *Communitas: The Anthropology of Collective Joy* (New York: Palgrave Macmillan, 2012), preface xi.
[101] Rosenwein, *Generations of Feeling*, p. 3.   [102] Turner, *Communitas*, pp. 1–2.

twentieth-century outdoor recreation organisations, and how this aim was enacted through their singing practices. We will explore how the fellowship engendered through open-air singing both opened-up and created limits to who could be part of these communities, and was extended to other-than-human aspects and actors in the landscape.

A desire to develop feelings of co-operation and fellowship amongst their members and a love and enjoyment of the open air were common foundational aims of many early twentieth-century outdoor recreation groups, including our focal groups founded in Northern England: the co-operative holiday movement and the SCR.[103] The CHA was founded in 1893 by Thomas Arthur Leonard, who also founded its sister organisation, the HF, in 1913. CHA and HF holidays aimed to 'give scope for the exercise of personality and initiative, but with everyone contributing to a common stock of fellowship and goodwill' where guests could discover 'the joys of fellowship in the open air'.[104] Similarly, the SCR, founded by George Herbert Bridges Ward in 1900, also aimed to foster a spirit of open-air fellowship, as the quote which opened this section indicated. Both Ward and Leonard were prominent figures in the leadership of open-air recreation; for instance, Leonard was the first president of the Ramblers' Association and Ward played a central role in wider campaigns for public access to the countryside.[105] Ward drew from a form of secular socialism and the collective struggle for access, whereas Leonard was influenced by his background as a congregational minister alongside the work of socialist thinkers to encourage fostering a belief in 'world brotherhood'.[106] However, both held a common ethos that taking part in communal activities and experiences – such as rambling, learning, singing and holidaying together – were ways of building both an individual's character and the bonds between people.

Singing together was seen as a medium well-suited to foster these bonds. The foreword to the CHA and HF joint songbook *Songs of Faith, Nature*

---

[103] A brief introduction to the co-operative holiday movement, the Sheffield Clarion Ramblers, and their contexts in relation to singing, is provided in Abbi Flint, 'Songs for Ramblers and Songs by the Way: Paths and Trails as Vernacular Contexts for Singing in the Early Twentieth Century', *Folklore* (2025).

[104] Gregory, 'T.A. Leonard', p. 644 and p. 646.

[105] See, for example, accounts of Ward's life and contribution to public access to the countryside in Holt, *G.H.B Ward 1876–1957*, and David Sissons, *A Sheffield Clarion Rambler: Some Aspects of the Life and Work of G. H. B. Ward (1876–1957)* (unpublished MA Thesis, University of Sheffield, 1992).

[106] Further information of the life and work of Thomas Arthur Leonard and specifically the co-operative holiday movement can be found in Robert Snape, 'The Co-operative Holidays Association and the Cultural Formation of Countryside Leisure Practice', *Leisure Studies*, 23: 2 (2004), 143–158, and Hope, 'The Democratisation of Tourism in the English Lake District', 105–126. See also, Thomas A. Leonard, 'Farewell', *Comradeship*, 6: 1, (September 1913) p. 4 on the ethos of the CHA.

and Fellowship described communal singing as a 'wonderfully unifying influence'.[107] Chorus singing was described in an earlier songbook edited by Henry Walford Davies as 'the very affirmation of good fellowship'.[108] A 1915 piece in the CHA magazine *Comradeship* emphasised the 'value of song in seasons of stress' such as wartime, and its power to encourage feelings of connection between people and to change their emotional state: 'music shares with the open air the power of refreshing and inspiring us, of rekindling enthusiasm and promoting good fellowship'.[109] Singing also lent language and metaphor to describe fellowship and community, for instance, as within a scouting movement songbook: 'a crowd of individuals working in harmony'.[110] Writing of communitas developed through music specifically, Edith Turner noted it as a distinctive form of human experience that goes beyond the individual, physical boundaries of our bodies through connecting through both rhythm, song and even a state of flow:

> In music, you join your voices completely, you are joined, you are in the same place, because you have gone altogether into the sound, and the sound is one sound with all the other people in it: one, in the same space.[111]

As noted in Section 1, recent scientific work has suggested that there are complex physical and social reasons underpinning senses of wellbeing and connection through singing. For instance, Camlin et al. described a blurring of the self and other, through group singing as a process of dialogue and negotiation, as one of the attributes of music that studies have indicated enables the development of interpersonal bonds.[112] For those singing in the open air, these feelings of connection extended to the landscapes in which they sung and recognised the role of the landscape in facilitating these social connections.[113] There are, of course, differences between these contemporary studies and the early twentieth century outdoor groups we are concerned with. For our outdoor recreation groups, open-air singing was just one part of their activities, and perhaps in a more informal sing-song than a choir-like setting.

In the early twentieth century, the collective singing encouraged by outdoor recreation groups was influenced by and set in the context of a national community singing movement in England, which was framed by some contemporary

---

[107] The CHA and HF, *Songs of Faith, Nature and Fellowship* (Co-operative Heritage Trust, CHA/3/2).
[108] Henry Walford Davies, *The Fellowship Songbook* (Liverpool: Rushworth and Dreaper, 1915), p.vi.
[109] Anon, 'The Fellowship Songbook', *Comradeship,* 9:2, p. 11.
[110] Vera Barclay, ed, *Campfire Singing for Scouts and Guides* (London: Novello, 1934) p. 10.
[111] Turner, *Communitas*, p. 48.
[112] Camlin et al., 'Group Singing as a Resource for the Development of a Healthy Public'.
[113] *Ibid.*

organisers and commentators as an antidote to post–First World War economic depression, class tensions and industrial unrest.[114] Large-scale community singing events were held in public spaces and high-profile venues such as the Albert Hall in London, with sponsorship from national newspapers, and numerous songbooks published.[115] John Goss, writing in the foreword to the Daily Express Community Song Book, described it as 'an astounding social movement that has since swept over the country like a prairie fire'.[116] Open-air elements of this movement included singing at football grounds, which

> were turned into gigantic open-air concert centres. Twenty, thirty, forty, fifty thousand men and women provided unforgettable spectacles as they stood in wintry sunshine or biting wind to sing sea shanties, old, well-known choruses, and – most memorable of all – 'God Save the King'.[117]

Therefore, communal singing was a practice many people may have enjoyed outside of these outdoor groups and that was promoted as a means to heal perceived social divisions during the 1920s.[118] The community singing movement was an inspiration not only for the notion of singing as a way of building togetherness but in terms of the type of songs perceived as most suitable to foster this. Community songbooks tended to include a mixture of patriotic, national, folk and popular songs. As Baden Powell stated in the 1947 introduction to the scouting movement's *Open Air Songbook*:

> These are the songs with which we began the community singing idea, and I remember hearing a thousand boys sing a dozen or so of them to the King and Queen at a Melba Concert in the Albert Hall in London.[119]

Other songs were chosen by outdoor recreation groups because they were perceived to evoke the spirit and emotions of fellowship when sung together. The foreword of the HF songbook, *Songs by the Way*, indicated that the selection of folksongs within the book was not made solely on aesthetic grounds but because they had 'a peculiar character of jollity which renders them particularly suitable for fellowship singing'.[120] The structure of some songs also reflected a focus on collective singing. For instance, songs were sometimes arranged in parts and some songbooks included rounds and call-and-response songs, which

---

[114] Roud, *Folk Song in England*, p. 418.
  Dave Russell, 'Abiding Memories: The Community Singing Movement and English Social Life in the 1920s', *Popular Music* 27: 1 (2008), pp. 117–133.
[115] For more on community singing see Russell, 'Abiding Memories'.
[116] John Goss (ed.), *'Daily Express' Community Song Book* (London: The London Express Newspaper, 1927).
[117] Ibid.   [118] Ibid.   [119] Poyser (ed), *The Open Air Songbook*, no page number.
[120] The Holiday Fellowship, *Songs by the Way* (London: The Holiday Fellowship, no date), foreword.

Figure 4 Cover of *The Mountain Club Songbook* (1955) featuring a hand-drawn cartoon of a mountaineer in the foreground facing a range of tall mountains. Credit: Licensed from the English Folk Dance and Song Society.

suggested group rather than individual singing. For example, the SCR song 'Up the Hill O' (to the tune of the folksong 'Twanky Dillo') had verses assigned for male and female voices separately before a final verse for all to sing together.[121]

Within the historical songbooks, there is also a sense that the groups themselves were tapping into existing practices of and enthusiasm for open-air singing amongst their members. The introduction to the HF's *Songs by the Way* described how 'many of the songs have been sung by them on mountain tracks and field paths, until they have become traditional'.[122] Ward, too, described many songs within the SCR songbook as 'regularly sung by Sheffield and Manchester Ramblers in the open, on moorland, hill slope or summit', indicating this was to some extent an existing open-air repertoire and practice amongst communities of ramblers.[123] The idea of a living repertoire of songs enjoyed by specific groups is epitomised in the introduction to the (Stafford) Mountain Club's songbook from 1955 (see Figure 4). The editor

---

[121] Ward, *Songs for Ramblers to Sing on the Moorlands*, p. 6.
[122] Holiday Fellowship, *Songs by the Way*, London, foreword.
[123] Ward, *Songs for Ramblers to Sing on the Moorlands*, p. 1.

described only printing on one side of the pages so that more songs may be printed on these blank pages as they 'become known', without the need to reprint the full songbook. Members were also encouraged to add songs to these pages individually.[124] We might also tentatively see the selection of songs within the open-air songbooks as reflecting a specific sub-section of community singing; a community tramping and open-air repertoire.[125]

The singing practices of these groups were no doubt also influenced by group singing activities amongst the wider movements they were aligned with. Ward advertised the first SCR club ramble, which took place on 2 September 1900, in the pages of the Clarion newspaper. The Clarion itself published songbooks of appropriate songs for 'socialist organisations across the Kingdom'.[126] A recent exhibition at the John Rylands Library in Manchester described communal singing at meetings as 'an integral part of Clarion Life'.[127] The co-operative movement also published a range of songbooks, beyond those specifically for use on holidays.[128]

Many open-air recreation groups had an explicit aim of improvement for their members, underpinned by ideas of the value of the educational and rational use of leisure time for the betterment of both the individual and society. Even in some of Ward's lyrics to SCR songs this idea is foregrounded:

> So be a Clarion Rambler and learn to be a man,
> And never be a 'flapper' girl, but wander while you can.[129]

This civilising ideal was often set in the context of a perceived contrast between urban leisure and life (often depicted as unhealthy, senseless and sometimes immoral) with the healthy and enriching experience of countryside leisure: a contrast we explore more fully in the next section. These improvement aims were translated into practices and publications which aimed to influence their members thinking and behaviour, shaping a kind of open-air citizenship. For Ward, one of the purposes of rambling clubs, such as the SCR, was as a form of

---

[124] Anon, *The Mountain Club Song Book* (Self-published, 1955). Vaughn Williams Memorial Library, MP 30.6.
[125] See Flint, 'Songs for Ramblers and Songs by the Way' for a more detailed discussion of the notion of a tramping repertoire within open-air groups at this time.
[126] Georgia Pearce (ed), *The Clarion Songbook* (London: The Clarion Press, 1906). Foreword by Robert Blatchford.
[127] *Workers' Playtime: Culture & Community in Industrial Lancashire*, exhibition at the John Rylands Library, Manchester, 29 March to 9 September 2023. https://www.library.manchester.ac.uk/rylands/visit/events/workers-playtime/.
[128] For more on co-operative songbooks see Jane Donaldson, 'Don't Shut Up Like an Oyster! Song books in the Co-op archive'. *Co-operative Heritage Trust Blog Posts*, 23 October 2023. www.co-operativeheritage.coop/blog/dont-shut-up-like-an-oyster-song-books-in-the-co-op-archive.
[129] From Ward's lyrics to 'The Trespasser's Song', in Ward, *Songs for Ramblers to Sing on the Moorlands*, p. 5.

training in the ethos of rambling (and by implication the club itself) through the passing on of knowledge and skills from older and more experienced ramblers who 'guide their younger brethren on the way . . . in developing true personality and desire for Access with responsibility.'[130] Such groups were essential in Ward's view so that urban-folk could 're-learn how to play' and 'intelligently ramble, and not aimlessly "hike"'.[131] Each year, the SCR published a handbook that listed the scheduled rambles for that year accompanied by suggested readings, poems or songs. The handbooks also included a series of topical essays (often written by Ward himself) and updates on the activities of various other outdoor focused organisations such as the Council for the Preservation of Rural England and the Commons, Open Spaces and Footpaths Preservation Society. Alongside this, it was expected that every SCR ramble would include a song and reading in the open-air or at a refreshment stop. The open-air educational aspect of the CHA included talks and sermons during walks, which were the core element of CHA holidays. For example, a 1938 summer holiday programme book from the CHA details walking excursions of between eight and fourteen miles for each weekday of the holiday (with an optional walk on Wednesday).[132] The CHA magazine (*Comradeship*) included informative articles as well as association updates, and their holiday programmes included lists of recommended reading (including songbooks). In the introduction to *The Fellowship Songbook*, the links between singing, improvement and fellow-feeling are made clear:

> We have been vaguely aware of our great heritage of song, but have not fully realised how truly educative and ennobling that heritage is, nor how its common enjoyment can knit us together in bonds of fellowship.[133]

As singing was part of this improving offer, the choice of songs, and the way they should be sung, played a role in shaping the right kind of open-air fellow or citizen. For some groups this meant that many popular songs of the time were not considered to be appropriate, illustrated by the following quote from the scouting movement: 'Music-hall songs are not camp-fire items. The "sentimental song" is never suggested as a solo; cheap stuff from the Student's Songbook dies out of popularity.'[134] Ultimately, song choice was

---

[130] Anon, 'Access and National Parks', *Sheffield Clarion Ramblers Handbook 1948–49*, 125–130, p. 130.

[131] George Herbert Bridges Ward, 'Three Men of the Moors', *Sheffield Clarion Ramblers Handbook 1949–50*, p. 83.

[132] The Co-operative Holiday Association, *Summer Holidays in the Isle of Man (Peel). Programme, Songs Etc* (London: CHA, 1938). Sheffield City Archive X95 2007/42.

[133] Walford Davies, *The Fellowship Songbook*, p. v.

[134] Barclay, *Campfire Singing for Scouts and Guides*, p. 11.

not to be left up to the scouts or guides themselves as 'they have not been educated up to a good standard of taste' but should be chosen by the Leader as a way of shaping their taste in what was deemed to be an acceptable direction.[135] Similarly, the author of a 1915 article in *Comradeship* wished that 'more wisdom was exercised in the choice of songs by amateur singers', who opted for popular songs that were considered to have less 'artistic value'.[136] The SCR songbook is less prescriptive in the type of songs to be sung (although Ward described English folksongs as being particularly appropriate), but we can see the publication of songbooks, and the editorial decisions about what to include and exclude, as shaping the repertoires of these groups.[137]

Therefore, whilst the act of singing was framed as a way of developing community spirit and fellow-feeling generally, the choice of what (and how) to sing was a way of shaping individual behaviours and attitudes in line with the expected cultural norms within groups. This was also informed by aspirational ideas about wider open-air citizenship, and appropriate ways of being in the countryside, which we explore in Section 3.

2.1 Group Singing and Identities

The songbooks published by open-air recreation groups provided a community resource, a shared repertoire of songs, but it is through the act of collective singing itself that these contributed to fellow-feeling and group identity. In an oral history project, led by the Moors for the Future Partnership and the Peak District National Park Authority in 2012, Linda Crawley recalled singing as an integral part of the culture and practice of the Woodcraft Folk in the 1960s.[138] She compared this to a sense of being part of a singing family: 'we all sang, we sang on the moors, we sang on the bus, we sang when we were having our lunch,

---

[135] *Ibid.*   [136] Anon, 'The Fellowship Songbook', *Comradeship*, p. 11.

[137] A caveat to this is that outdoor recreation groups also had to obtain copyright permissions to reproduce songs and their lyrics, and introductions to some songbooks indicate this had meant some songs within their repertoires where not able to be included in published songbooks. See also Abbi Flint, 'Songs for Ramblers and Songs by the Way: Paths and Trails as Vernacular Contexts for Singing in the Early Twentieth Century', *Folklore* 136: 3 (2025), 490–515. doi:10.1080/0015587X.2025.2501423, for a more detailed discussion of the types of songs included in the SCR and CHA/HF songbooks, in particular their connections to folk song.

[138] The Woodcraft Folk are a youth-focused open-air movement, formed in 1925 by Leslie Paul, and broadly aligned with the co-operative movement. For further information see https://woodcraft.org.uk/about-woodcraft-folk/our-history/ and Sarah Mills, '"A Powerful Educational Instrument": The Woodcraft Folk and Indoor/Outdoor "Nature", 1925–75', in Sarah Mills and Peter Kraftl (eds), *Informal Education, Childhood and Youth* (London: Palgrave Macmillan, 2014), 65–78

we were like the von Trapp family singers sometimes'.[139] As a living tradition, songs were not just learned through songbooks but from others as a form of both peer and inter-generational learning:

> a lot of the time from the adults who'd grown up through the Woodcraft Folk, taught us the songs when we went to camps and things . . . and we always had music nights so we learned from each other and from the adults. So there was a history. And we had our songbooks.[140]

In a 1915 article for *Comradeship*, Henry Walford Davies described how songbooks themselves could facilitate these connections between people not just in the present but across time and generations:

> A song book is a human, not a musical document. Through its pages a lonely soul can converse with its kind; comrades can find fellowship; a present and harassed generation can exchange confidences with an age that is past, and find a steadying influence in an expression of feeling which is both free and orderly, both full of fantasy and full of method, at once whimsical and logical, refreshing the mind and the imagination of both the singer and his hearers.[141]

Here, the songbooks are framed as a way of accessing fellow-feeling at distance, away from the companionship and settings in which communal open-air singing took place. Singing these songs was an act of remembering others, reconnecting with memories of shared experiences, and also perhaps an expression of longing and nostalgia for the ideal of a comforting past. Writing in 1926, Stephen Graham reflects on the interplay between song, memory, emotions and identity, and how these are brought to the fore through rambling and singing together in the countryside:

> I'm singing. And singing what? Not the latest song, by any means, but something remembered from childhood and school days, the happy innocent strains of days gone by. Songs give birth to songs, memories to memories.[142]

Many of the founding members of the SCR were part of the Clarion Vocal Choir's Saturday rambling group and, therefore, were likely to have sung together already.[143] Indeed, singing was depicted as something to be celebrated and rewarded – one of Ward's 'hints' for ramblers in the club's 1919–20

---

[139] Linda Crawley in Moors for the Future, *Moor Memories Oral History Project: 'A living, working moorland'*, *Transcriptions of Interviews* (2012), p. 8. Derbyshire Records Office, D7534.
[140] Crawley in *Moor Memories*, p. 2.
[141] Henry Walford Davies, 'Our New Songbook', *Comradeship*, 9:1 (October 1915), 9–10, p. 10.
[142] Graham, *The Gentle Art of Tramping*, pp. 129–130.
[143] Dave Sissons, Terry Howard and Roly Smith, *Clarion Call: Sheffield's Access Pioneers* (Sheffield: Clarion Call Editorial Group, 2017), p. 71.

handbook suggested that 'should the Leader sing a jolly song, the party have permission to treat him to his tea'.[144] Group singing (and their shared repertoire) were also a way of identifying with the club. In an account of a ramble in 1921, a club member described the arrival of their founder, G.H.B Ward, announced through singing one of their club songs:

> Half way up the side of Bretton Clough we stopped for a breather, and were for a moment astonished at hearing the 'Land of Moor and Heather' being sung 'loud and clear' apparently from the clouds. Looking up, on a projecting cliff, and like an eagle in his eyrie, stood a form outlined against the blue sky, rucksack on back, and voice uplifted in melody.[145]

This was followed by a call and response of songs, with the resting ramblers singing one of the club songs back to Ward, who responded with a solo rendition of another club song ('A Jovial Tramp am I'). In this way, the songs provided an intra-community means of communicating connection in the landscape. On the same ramble after lunch the group sang more of their shared repertoire, outside the Barrel Inn at Bretton, 'to the evident amazement and, let us hope, pleasure of a few strangers who had halted for a modest refresher'.[146] It is clear from these descriptions that group singing was a well-rehearsed practice and a way of expressing their sense of togetherness when out rambling, in contrast with the 'strangers' they encountered in the countryside.

Another way that singing connected with group identity was through the circulation of new lyrics to existing tunes, which celebrated the exploits and characters of members of the SCR. For example, 'A Toasting Song', sung to the tune of the traditional song *John Peel*, included the following lines about the club's founder:

> D'ye ken Bert Ward, when he's out for the day,
> With boots like tanks and his mop of hair astray?[147]

Another song, 'The Sheepskin and the Jumper', gently pokes fun at the rambling attire of two club members: 'Whiteley's old grey jumper' and 'Diver's sheepskin jacket'.[148] Re-versioning songs was not a practice limited to the SCR; it also seems to have been common practice amongst members of various twentieth century climbing clubs. For example, the Manchester Rucksack Club's *The Songs of the Mountaineers,* published in 1922, included over forty club songs, which the editor, John Hirst, placed in a separated section: 'As a concession to readers on the fringe of our circle who may be a little aghast at

---

[144] Anon, 'Hints to Leaders', *Sheffield Clarion Ramblers Handbook 1919–20,* p. 120.
[145] The Wee Mon, 'Our Coming of Age Ramble', p. 59.   [146] *Ibid.*
[147] Ward, *Songs for Ramblers to Sing on the Moorlands,* p. 12.   [148] *Ibid,* p. 12 and p. 14.

our familiarities'.[149] However, it was not a practice shared or condoned across all open-air recreation groups. The scouting movement advised against re-writes arguing this 'spoils the tune forever; and the result is not any more fun to sing than real amusing songs and choruses'.[150]

Singing was also a way of cementing shared bonds of fellowship and identification within groups beyond their open-air activities and holidays. Group singing was part of CHA conference and reunion events, and the SCR sang together at their club dinners.[151] As T. Henderson noted in the pages of *Comradeship* in 1914, music itself was part of the fellowship of CHA holidays 'we make new friends not only of men and women, but of books and music'.[152]

2.2 Boundaries and Limits

Another common thread across the SCR and CHA was that the communal activities and notions of fellowship were open to men and women together – an ethos that was not universal across outdoor recreation organisations at this time. The scouting movement had separate groups for girls (rosebuds/brownies and guides) and boys (cubs and scouts), and many climbing clubs did not accept female members until later in the twentieth century. For instance, the Manchester based Rucksack Club only admitted women members from 1990.[153] Indeed, one of the distinctive characteristics of CHA and HF holidays was a notion of equal fellowship across gender and social standing, informed by a belief that 'irrespective of class, education or worldly possessions, the deepest joys are to be found in human friendship and fellowship'.[154] As Leonard wrote to CHA members in 1910:

> One of the best things that our movement offers is the possibility of frank and open friendships between men and women. On the tramp, and in the intercourse of the centre, there are the fullest opportunities for both to contribute to and share in the spiritual and intellectual life of the fellowship.[155]

The annual handbooks of the SCR indicated that women were involved (albeit to a much lesser extent than men) in the running of the club and leading some of the club's scheduled rambles in the early twentieth century. Furthermore, the

---

[149] John Hirst (ed), *The Songs of the Mountaineers* (Manchester: W. Allen Corner, 1922), no page number.
[150] Barclay, *Campfire Singing for Scouts and Guides*, p. 15.
[151] Scriptor, 'Manchester 1938', *Comradeship*, 29: 3 (Spring 1938), 9–11, p. 9.
[152] T. Henderson, 'What Shall I Sing?' *Comradeship*, 7:5 (May 1914), p. 69.
[153] See the Rucksack Club's webpage here for more on their history https://rucksackclub.org/who-we-are/club-history/.
[154] Anon, 'Extracts from Our Forty-Fifth Annual Report', *Comradeship* 29:3, (Spring 1938), 11–14, p. 11.
[155] T. A. Leonard, 'To Our Members', *Comradeship*, 4:3 (December 1910), 35–36, p. 35.

exploits and characters of female members of the club were celebrated in the lyrics of some songs in their songbook:

> Hilda, she's a sturdy lass; Mrs Bingley is as well;
> It's a treat to see them going, over moor and fell.[156]

However, there were still activities that were off-limits to women members. Women were asked not to take part in some of the club's hardiest outings, including some Midnight Rambles and winter Revellers Rambles, and it was not until 1955 that the first formal women's Revellers Ramble took place.[157]

Whilst not mentioning singing specifically, the historian Melanie Tebbutt has suggested that the incorporation of poetry and literature within Ward's ethos for the SCR spoke to a 'need for emotional release more usually constrained by the conventions and expectations of contemporary manliness' and an alternative, more complex, expression of masculinity.[158] Whilst rambling on the rugged hills and bleak moorlands of the Peak District was associated with more traditional ideas of masculinity, for Ward this was tempered by a very different manly expression of feeling through song and brotherly companionship with his fellow (male) ramblers, informed by Romanticism and the socialist writing of his friend Edward Carpenter. This combination of nature, song and manly companionship could be powerfully moving, as this extract from the 1916–17 SCR handbook, cited by Dave Sissons, Terry Howard and Roly Smith, illustrates. It was written by club member Harry Inman about walking with G. H. B Ward:

> We sang – he and I. Yes, you stay-at-home heathens. I repeat – we sang. His deep resonant voice betraying his emotions. He revelled, he jumped, he shouted and danced to his heart's content; then he did what only a nature-loving man can do. He wept. Great tears welled into his eyes as his arms went around my neck.[159]

When writing about fellow-feeling, publications from both the CHA and SCR refer to this in masculine terms. For example, in a piece about 'our coming of age ramble', the author (The Wee Mon) described 'the same old Clarionese spirit of brotherliness'.[160] Similarly, in an article from *Comradeship*, T. A. Leonard described the CHA and HF as providing 'simple fraternal holidays'.[161] Whilst these possibly reflect writing styles of the time (where the masculine was taken to

---

[156] Taken from 'Snapshots', lyrics by H. H. Diver and sung to the tune of 'The Derby Ram', from Ward, *Songs for Ramblers to Sing on the Moorlands,* p. 21.
[157] Sissons et al., *Clarion Call* Anon, 'Women Reveller – Ramblers', *Sheffield Clarion Ramblers Handbook 1955–56,* p. 130.
[158] Melanie Tebbutt, 'Rambling and Manly Identity in Derbyshire's Dark Peak, 1880s–1920s', *The Historical Journal,* 49: 4 (2006), 1125–53, p. 1153.
[159] Sissons et al., *Clarion call,* p. 42. [150] The Wee Mon, 'Our Coming of Age Ramble', p. 57.
[161] Leonard, 'Farewell', p. 4.

represent all people), there are further pieces that explore the expression of ideas of 'manly' and 'gentlemanly' ways of being in the context of behaviour in the countryside and at holiday centres. We will come back to this theme in Section 3.

Just as the wider activities of groups like the SCR sometimes reflected inequalities in the reach of fellow-feeling along lines of gender, their open-air singing practices and associated publications reflected a fellowship that was perhaps not universally welcoming. The selection of songs across the historical songbooks, for instance, suggests possibilities for both inclusion and exclusion. The CHA and HF songbooks included sections of hymns which may have been unfamiliar to those who weren't of Christian faith. As already noted, the SCR songbook included many rewritten songs, referencing the exploits of members of the club itself. One can imagine these may have been experienced as cliquey and less than welcoming by new members. Some iterations of songbooks from the co-operative holiday movement included songs made popular through blackface minstrelsy. Although popular with some audiences at the time, we now understand these as perpetuating harmful stereotypes of blackness and they must be considered in the broader context of complex histories of the othering and marginalisation of people from global majority backgrounds within rural landscapes and outdoor recreation.[162]

There is also some evidence that songbooks (and the songs within them) were employed to promote aspirations for fellow-feeling beyond the groups they originally served. In contrast to the perhaps inward-looking and national focus of the community singing movement, some aspects of the singing practices of outdoor recreation groups served to extend fellow-feeling beyond national borders. CHA songbooks were requested (and in some cases supplied free-of-charge) by soldiers in military camps during the First World War.[163] Even earlier, a 1912 issue of the CHA magazine *Comradeship* described how 'demand for our songbook increases yearly' and copies had been sent to a missionary-led School in Africa: 'thus the circle of our influence widens'.[164] In addition, song selection sometimes indicated international connections. Another outdoor recreation holiday organisation, International Tramping Tours, which T.A. Leonard was involved in forming in the 1930s, included numerous songs from other nations in their songbook, sometimes in languages other than English so that there was 'no excuse for not joining in when our

---

[162] Aayushi Bajwala, 'Walking on the Margin: A Study of Marginalised Ethnic Groups and Their Walking Practices in Urban and Rural Britain', *Field*, 8:1 (2022), 169–186, p. 177. Paul Cloke, 'Rurality and Racialised Others: Out of Place in the Countryside?' in Neil Chakraborti and Jon Garland, eds, *Rural Racism* (Cullompton: Willan, 2004), 17–35. p. 23.

[163] Anon, 'Our Songbook', *Comradeship*, 8:2 (December 1914), p. 3.

[164] Anon, 'Tunebook', *Comradeship*, 5:5 (April 1912), p. 67.

friends abroad are singing'.[165] Whilst the SCR songbook did not include songs from other countries, articles within their handbook suggested they welcomed, and celebrated, 'foreign' members in a spirit of 'international brotherhood', including visitors from Egypt, India and Germany.[166]

2.3 Fellow-feeling with Nature

In the foreword to the SCR songbook, Ward described one purpose of the book as 'the emulation of the birds who give praise to Nature by their full-throated, joyous song'.[167] This evoked a form of fellow-feeling with nature: with other-than-human actors and dimensions of the countryside. A similar comparison was made in the introduction to a scouting songbook: 'Nature expresses itself in music and song. Scouts can follow Nature's example.'[168] Both of these examples also emphasise how this fellow-feeling was brokered through an emotional connection and the expression of these emotions through song. Through singing people actively responded to and contributed to emotional, imaginative and sensory encounters with the other-than-human. As the historian Michael Guida has highlighted:

> the natural world could itself provoke the rambler into making their own sounds, to complement walking rhythms or to celebrate a sense of freedom, and this contribution to the soundscape should be considered as part of a wide-ranging sensory interplay of body and mind with outdoor surroundings.[169]

There was a sense that, if done in the right way and choosing the right songs, open-air singing complemented and was in harmony with the natural elements of these soundscapes. The example that opened this Element – describing evening singing around a campfire on a CHA holiday – illustrated this with the human voices portrayed as 'fitting delightfully' with 'the whisper of the wind and the beck's bright flowing chatter'.[170]

The other-than-human is also represented in some of the lyrics of songs included in open-air songbooks. For instance, 'The Clarion Ramblers'

---

[165] Anon, *International Tramping Tours Songbook*. Leeds: International Tramping Tours (no date), p. 2. See also Douglas Hope, *Whatever Happened to 'Rational' Holidays for Working People c.1919–2000? The Competing Demands of Altruism and Commercial Necessity in the Co-operative Holidays Association and Holiday Fellowship*. Doctoral thesis, University of Cumbria (2015).
[166] George H. B. Ward, '"Foreign" S.C.R. members', *Sheffield Clarion Ramblers Handbook 1949–50*, pp. 67–8.
[167] Ward, *Songs for Ramblers to Sing on the Moorlands*, p. 1.
[168] J. S. Wilson in Barclay, *Campfire Singing for Scouts and Guides*, p. 3.
[169] Michael Guida, *Listening to British Nature: Wartime, Radio, and Modern Life, 1914–1945* (New York: Oxford University Press, 2022), p. 116.
[170] Anon, 'A Holiday Experience', pp. 15–16.

Marching Song' (with new words by H. H. Diver set to the tune of 'When Johnny Comes Marching Home') places the ramblers in northern moors, with attention to many natural aspects of this rural setting, including sounds. The song mentions heather, 'mountain sheep', grouse, cotton grass, rivers, and 'where raging torrents roar' and 'where the birds' sweet music trills', and described how

> Far away from the city crowd,
> Alone with Nature we shout aloud.[171]

There are less bespoke songs in *Songs by the Way*, but the selection of religious and folk songs often include references to rural and countryside environments, and in some cases, the sense of harmony between human and natural society. For instance, 'In Derry Vale', references 'the singing river' in the opening line, and 'The Hunt is Up' describes the response of nature to the sound of the hunting horns:

> The grasse is greene and so are the treene,
> All laughing at the sound
> The horses snort to be at the sport,
> The dogges are running free,
> The woddes rejoyce at the merie noise Of hey tantara tee ree![172]

All of these give the sense of open-air singing as part of mingled rural soundscapes, although these examples indicate perceptions of the countryside as a largely unpopulated space for nature – (something we explore further in Section 3.1). The notion of singing as a point of connection between human and the other-than-human perhaps also connects with older traditions of singing amongst agricultural workers, as described by folklorist Steve Roud, which included milkmaids singing to cows to calm them and encourage milk yield and the chanting of bird-scaring rhymes.[173]

Along with fellow-feeling amongst the men and women who were members of outdoor recreation groups, and building a feeling of connection with nature generally, there were elements of fellowship through open-air singing which were specifically rooted in the rural landscapes that these groups knew and loved. It is these connections with place that we explore in the next section.

3 Relating to Place

Sing them upon the sunny hills
When the days are long and bright.[174]

---

[171] Ward, *Songs for Ramblers to Sing on the Moorlands*, p. 18.
[172] Holiday Fellowship, *Songs by the Way*, p. 8, p. 33.
[173] Roud, *Folk Song in England*, p. 539.
[174] Extract from a poem by Felicia Dorothea Hemans, from the cover of The Holiday Fellowship, *Songs by the Way* (tunebook) (London: Holiday Fellowship, 1923).

The individual voice and the various communities of singers with their songbooks were also rooted in and responded to specific places. In this section we will focus on the interplay between a local region, the north of England, and the open-air singing practices of the SCR and the co-operative holiday movement. The SCR had a strong connection with the moorlands extending out of Sheffield and into parts of Derbyshire (which although strictly part of the East Midlands region has much in common with the Northern landscape, particularly the sections containing parts of the Peak District). Although it was a national movement the co-operative holiday movement had links with the English Lake District: their first holiday centre was a converted graphite mill in Stair, near Keswick. Many Lake District and Derbyshire fells and paths would therefore have resounded with the songs of early twentieth century ramblers. We chose these groups as they encouraged singing in the countryside as part of their activities, and published collections of songs specifically to be sung in these landscapes. This purpose is implicit in the titles and cover illustrations of these publications. For example, the SCR songbook was titled *Songs for Ramblers to Sing on the Moorlands* (see Figure 1) and the HF songbook, *Songs by the Way*, included a reference to paths ('the Way') in its title. The 1923 tunebook for *Songs by the Way* featured an inviting pastoral scene of a group of figures, in capes and hats, walking alongside the tree-lined shore of a lake, the sun peeping over the distant mountains on the far shore (see Figure 5). One of the figures (on the left) has stopped with an open book; perhaps representing the songbook itself?

The introductory text within songbooks also indicated that the songs had been selected 'because they are suitable for singing in the open air', along paths and in upland and rural landscapes.[175] Other publications by these organisations described singing in rural landscapes in accounts of group activities. For example, on a club trip to the Lake District the SCR sang the club song 'Land of Moor and Heather' on the summit of Helvellyn.[176] Similarly, an article in *Comradeship* from February 1913, recalled a CHA group ramble up Great Gable, also in the Lake District, with the ramblers singing on the summit in thick fog.[177]

The small size of many of the songbooks published by outdoor recreation groups, including the SCR, CHA and International Tramping Tours, enabled portability and ensured they could be taken out into the landscapes where they were intended to be sung. In relation to the *Open Air Songbook* of the scouting

---

[175] The Holiday Fellowship, *Fellowship Holidays,* foreword.
[176] Anon, 'The 1919 Whitsuntide (Climbing) Week', p. 99.
[177] J. T. G., 'Rapture in the Rain', *Comradeship*, 6:4 (February 1913), p. 64.

Figure 5 Cover of the 1923 Holiday Fellowship tunebook, *Songs by the Way*. Credit: HF Holidays Limited.

movement, Baden Powell said he 'should like to have its pocket edition in every haversack and then in every camper's hand when supper is ended and the camp fire is aglow'.[178]

Whilst our focus is open-air recreational singing in the twentieth century, we acknowledge that this connects with longer histories of singing outdoors in English rural landscapes, often in relation to work. For example, the songs sung by agricultural workers on the land, at home and at union meetings in the nineteenth century or those sung whilst working in cottage industries like straw-plaiting outdoors.[179] Unions for rural workers also published their own

---

[178] Poyser, *The Open Air Songbook*, no page number.
[179] Roy Palmer, *The Painful Plough* (Cambridge: Cambridge University Press, 1973) and Roud, *Folk Song in England*, p. 534.

songbooks to be used at their meetings.[180] As Steve Roud has noted, singing at work was not just about rhythm; people sang for many reasons: 'to cheer themselves up, pass the time, foster community feeling, have a laugh, show off their singing skills, tease each other and mock outsiders or those in charge, protest their conditions.'[181] There is also a localised example of open-air community singing specific to some villages on the outskirts of Sheffield and in Derbyshire, which may have been known to the SCR: the long-standing tradition of secular singing of local Christmas carols outside homes, on village streets and in public houses. This is a living, vernacular practice, which has strong place-based elements, including different repertoires of carols sung in specific locations and many titles of carols relating to local places, such as 'Malin Bridge'. Ian Russell has described how participants in local carol 'sings' gained a sense of wellbeing, built relationships, and could express themselves freely and informally through 'a special spiritual song that resonates with place'.[182] Although these represent distinctly different traditions of outdoor singing, there are common threads in the interplay between rural environments, community and song.

In this section we consider the role of sound (and specifically singing) in the development of a sense of place, and connectedness with place during the early and mid-twentieth century. All of this is set in the context of decades of contested access to what were perceived as open or public spaces from the nineteenth century. As the historian of science Anne Secord has noted:

> Place assumed immense cultural and political importance in the nineteenth century as space itself became class specific. Enclosure, the game laws, and the geographical demarcation of towns like Manchester effectively excluded the poor from space that was formerly public.[183]

There has been considerable scholarly discussion about the concept of place across diverse disciplines, and it is not our intention here to summarise this complex and wide-ranging debate. However, in the context of this Element it is useful to highlight the role that sound plays in how people connect with and conceptualise places. The anthropologist Clifford Geertz has argued that the

---

[180] E.g. Anon, *National Agricultural Labourers' and Rural Workers' Union Songbook* (Maddermarket, Norwich: Caxton Press, c.1916).
[181] Roud, *Folk Song in England,* p. 529.
[182] Ian Russell, 'Vernacular Christmas Carol Singing in the Southern Pennines of England', in Esther M. Morgan-Ellis and Kay Norton, *The Oxford Handbook of Community Singing* (Oxford: Oxford University Press, 2024), pp. 161–182.
[183] Ann Secord, 'Science in the Pub: Artisan Botanists in Early Nineteenth-Century Lancashire', *History of Science* 32: 97 (1994), 269–315, p. 275.

idea of place is important because 'no one lives in the world in general'.[184] Drawing on phenomenological perspectives, place can be an idea that holds the complex physical, psychical, historical, cultural, social and natural dimensions and meanings of environments.[185] Experiences of place blend the cognitive, emotional and embodied, an important part of which includes perception through the senses. Sense and place are reciprocal and entangled, as the anthropologist and enthnomusicologist Steven Feld has argued: 'as place is sensed, senses are placed; as places make sense, senses make place'.[186] Feld draws attention to the dominance of the visual in much scholarship on sense of place and landscape, and uses the term 'acoustemology' to express the idea that a sense of place can also be 'grounded in an acoustic dimension'.[187] Stocker has argued that sound is integral to our sense of being 'in place'. Making sound is a way of expressing who we are in relation to place and hearing and feeling the 'soundscapes we are within' contributes to our subjective (and emotional) experience of place: 'The world enters us by way of sound – we sound back to gauge where we are in the world.'[188] This emphasises that sonic aspects of place are co-created by people alongside other human and other-than-human elements of environments. Constructions and meanings of specific places draw on both the sounds heard and the associations, experiences and emotions they inspire, and the sounds people make themselves. 'Places may come into presence through the experience of bodily sensation, but it is through expression that they reach heightened emotional and aesthetic dimensions or sensual inspiration.'[189] Thus, singing in the landscape contributes to both expressions and senses of place.

Drawing on these ideas of the connections between sound and place-making, we explore the role of singing in wider co-created rural soundscapes, which already included diverse sonic dimensions, in the mid-twentieth century. These can be related to specific ideals and conceptions of the countryside during this period which influenced how sound, as an aspect of people's ways of being in the landscape, was configured in the context of outdoor leisure.

3.1 Sensing the 'Countryside' and the Rural

Open-air leisure in the late nineteenth and early twentieth century was often framed as a way of escaping the town or city: 'Rambling is, to the rambler,

---

[184] Clifford Geertz, 'Afterword', in S. Feld and K. Basso (eds) *Senses of Place* (Santa Fe: School of American Research Press, 2011), 259–262, p. 259.
[185] Edward S. Casey, 'How to Get from Space to Place in a Fairly Short Stretch of Time', in S. Feld and K. Basso (eds), *Senses of Place* (Santa Fe: School of American Research Press, 2011), pp. 13–52.
[186] Feld, 'Waterfalls of Song', p. 91.   [187] Feld, 'Waterfalls of Song', p. 97.
[188] Stocker, *Hear Where We Are*.   [189] Feld, 'Waterfalls of Song', p. 134.

a **conscious escape** from High streets to Hills, from Monotony to Moors, from Noise to Nature' (emphasis in original).[190] The countryside was defined in opposition to the urban and the industrial – offering clean air, space, tranquillity in noise and pace of life, and the potential for embodied connection with nature through healthy physical exercise. As cultural geographer David Matless has outlined, the idea of a 'landscaped citizenship' in the early twentieth century was defined in opposition to an idea of vulgar, anti-citizenship – epitomised by out-of-place urban behaviours – and rooted in an inherent 'desire to control potentially disruptive bodily effects'.[191] Numerous articles in the SCR handbooks from the early and mid-twentieth century included complaints about out-of-place town behaviours (and by association town people) in the countryside. Explicit in this is a contrast between the influences of the urban versus the rural on the moral character of individuals and its implications for wider society; spending time in the countryside and connecting with nature were portrayed as benefiting both physical and spiritual health, allowing people a more natural and authentic sense of self:[192]

> The finest virility comes not from town and its mob spectators but from constant contact with nature wild and free.[193]

There is also a sense of timelessness in this characterisation of the countryside, in which perceived 'natural' soundscapes played their part:

> The very sounds of life – the whistle of the curlew, the bleating of the mountain sheep – add to the sense of primeval solitude. To these sounds the crags have echoed for a thousand and ten thousand years; to these sounds and to the rushing of the winds and the waters they will echo ten thousand years hence.[194]

In reality, however, the twentieth-century English countryside was not exempt from the influence of modernity. It was a collection of working and lived-in landscapes, with soundscapes comprising entangled human and other-than-human dimensions. As Michael Guida reminds us, this included singing:

> What should be noted here is that the countryside, with its age-old soundscape, would have also resounded with the modern sounds of songs brought

---

[190] Sidney F. Wicks, 'A Reverie', in Manchester Ramblers' Federation, *The Rambler's Handbook* 1927, p. 14.
[191] David Matless, *Landscape and Englishness* (London: Reaktion Books, 2016), p. 95.
[192] *Ibid.*
[193] George H. B. Ward, 'Three Men of the Moors', *Sheffield Clarion Ramblers Handbook* 1949–50, 83, p. 84.
[194] Alpha of the Plough, 'In praise of walking', in Manchester Ramblers' Federation, *The Rambler's Handbook* 1923, p. 20.

from the human world of dancing, working, and fighting. And part of the sonic culture of walking in nature was as much about marking out a rhythm or a tune as it was listening to a bird in song.[195]

Histories of the perceptions of soundscapes in rural environments have received less scholarly study that those in urban settings, but the descriptions found in texts and oral histories provide some insights into these.[196] A partial portrait of the complex soundscapes of the countryside between Sheffield and Manchester can be drawn from oral history accounts of living and working in the South Pennine moorlands in the mid and later twentieth century, collected as part of the *Moor Memories* project.[197] These accounts illustrated how the moors were far from quiet: with various sounds contributed by farming, military training, industrial exploitation, the work of mountain rescue and ranger/warden teams, and game shooting. Each of these activities brought distinctive noises that formed part of the sensory experience of being in these landscapes.

During the Second World War, moorland access for leisure was limited because of military use of the moors for training. This brought with it a range of sonic elements including the sounds of the troops themselves, vehicles and heavy machinery such as tanks, and from target practice, often with live ammunition. They were also sites of bombing and plane crashes, which brought distinctive sounds (along with sights, smells and potentially upsetting encounters with casualties):

> We were getting bracken one day on the moor and this plane came over very low, tut-tut-tut-tut-tutting, and then there was a crash and we set off. Well, I'd travelled about another mile and a half by the time we got there. Anyway the young fella was dead by the time we got there. It wasn't on fire or anything so of course we came home and reported it.[198]

The sonic impact of military activities resounded long after the war ended; live munitions remained on the moors and contributed to soundscapes when detonated by bomb disposal teams or set off accidentally – as John Littlewood describes in relation to an incident during controlled burning.[199] The locations

---

[195] Guida, *Listening to British Nature*, p. 115.
[196] Wilko Graf von Hardenberg and Anne Hehl, 'Environmental Echoes: Finding Historical Soundscapes of Nature in Textual Sources', *Journal of Literature and Science*, 17: 2 (2024), pp. 78–92.
[197] For an introduction to this project see www.moorsforthefuture.org.uk/__data/assets/pdf_file/0032/87548/Moor-Memories-Booklet.pdf.
[198] Ray Platts in Moors for the Future, *Moor Memories*, p. 9.
[199] John Littlewood in Moors for the Future, *Moor Memories*, p. 12.

of unexploded shells and bombs were often noticed by hikers and workers in the landscape and their detonation could have dramatic effects:

> I met the bomb disposal people at snake summit. And we walked in and we found the location. And he said, 'Yes, I'm going to blow this here'. So he put this plastic on it, and all the rest of it. He said, 'You go away' so I went away, I went onto some high ground. He said, 'Just make sure there's nobody around and I'll join you'. Anyway, he lit the fuse, or whatever he did with it, he walked about 10 yards away from this mortar – bear in mind the fuse is burning – stopped, got a fag out, lit the fag and walked nonchalantly to where I was and – BOOM! – the whole thing went up![200]

As a working landscape, technologies of labour and transportation were also part of these soundscapes. For instance, Peak Park Rangers and Mountain Rescue Teams described using flare guns to communicate across distance in the landscape. Heavy industry such as quarrying and mining introduced industrial noises into the landscape. For example, John Littlewood described using gelignite (explosive) whilst working in a clay-mine as a young man.[201] The mid-twentieth-century rise in popularity of motorcycles presented a new challenge not only in the potential for physical harm to both landscapes and other path-users but in terms of a sonic assault from 'the racket of their engines'.[202] In a piece on trial-motorcyclists in Derbyshire, Ward wrote, 'we always like sport, but we love Peace better than War-noise on God's good hills'.[203]

Outdoor leisure itself brought new dimensions to countryside soundscapes. Post-war, and after the 1949 National Parks and Access to the Countryside Act was passed, the numbers of people going out into the countryside to walk swelled. The sound of these group rambles would have been immense; Guida cited an account from a South Shields MP suggesting there may have been as many as 800 people on Southern Railway rambles.[204] The impact of these crowds was not limited to moors and hillsides. Many people made their way into the countryside by public transport meaning that people congregated at the same time in cafes and around train and bus stops, and noise – including singing and rhythmic stamping of hobnailed walking boots – continued on buses and trains:[205]

---

[200] Ian Hurst, Peak Park Rangers first interview in Moors for the Future, *Moor Memories*, p. 23.
[201] John Littlewood in Moors for the Future, *Moor Memories*, p. 16.
[202] 'Wanderbird', 'A New Invasion of the Hills', *Northern Rambler*, 1: 1 (October 1935), p. 6.
[203] George H. B. Ward, 'Motor Cyclists "Access"', *Sheffield Clarion Ramblers Handbook 1955–56*, 121–123, p. 123.
[204] Guida, *Listening to British Nature*.
[205] Ken Drabble in Moors for the Future, *Moor Memories*, p. 1.

There was an explosion of people wanting to come out into Derbyshire. And, for instance, the platforms of Edale station of an evening would be absolutely heaving with people.[206]

Whilst the numbers of people on rambles in the earlier twentieth century may not have been in the region of 800, photographs of SCR members in the landscape showed large group rambles (for instance, a photograph held by Sheffield City Archive shows eighty-one men and women on their thirtieth-anniversary ramble in 1930) and CHA holiday centres typically accommodated between fifty and seventy people.[207] These large groups would have significantly contributed to the sounds of the countryside when talking and singing on rambles.

In the early days of the Peak District National Park, *Byelaws for behaviour on access land* were issued, one of which related to the use of 'transistor radios and noisy instruments' and forbid people to 'make of cause or suffer to be made any noise which is so loud and so continuous or repeated as to give reasonable cause for annoyance to other persons on access land'.[208] However, there was a subjective element in how these were interpreted and enforced in practice:

> On one occasion somebody had complained ... at being told off by a warden for playing their transistor radio loudly. And they'd pointed up there and said, 'What about that guy up there who's playing bagpipes?' [laughing] 'Ah well, it was in the right place', [warden] would say [laughing].[209]

New technologies brought new sensorial dimensions to the landscape which were not universally welcomed and heightened tensions between different groups enjoying the countryside in different ways. Traditional instruments and singing may have been tolerated, but technologically amplified music was frowned upon and grouped with other forms of behaviour deemed to be anti-social: 'Nice people who wouldn't dream of leaving litter about or carving their names on trees can be dreadfully anti-social by assaulting us with transistor radios in the Centres and even on excursions!'[210] Concerns around the impact of modern technologies on rural landscapes continued into the later twentieth century, with the CHA magazine noting that 'Noise problems grow worse' in 1980:

> Have you ever thought that it is becoming more and more difficult to find peace and quiet in the countryside? Agricultural machinery, transistor radios,

---

[206] Bill Garlick, Peak Park Rangers first interview in Moors for the Future, *Moor Memories*, p. 5.
[207] Hope, *Whatever Happened to 'Rational' Holidays for Working People*.
[208] Peak Park Planning Board, *Byelaws for Behaviour on Access Land* (1964). Derbyshire Records Office, D4721/10/1.
[209] Peak Park Rangers second interview in Moors for the Future, *Moor Memories*, p. 35
[210] Anon, 'Noises off – and on', *Comradeship*, 52:4 (Winter 1962), p. 27.

power boats all seem to get louder and louder and ramblers have to go further and further into the wilds to escape from them.[211]

Here, the landscape sought out by ramblers is an idealised countryside: a tranquil place, sensorially free from all signs of contemporary (and especially urban or industrial) society.

3.2 Contested Ways of Being in the Countryside

These examples illustrate how, across the twentieth century, some sensorial dimensions have been welcomed and expected, whereas others were perceived as out of place, and in discord – rather than in harmony – with ideal or appropriate countryside soundscapes. Attempts to regulate or constrain singing (and other sounds) in the countryside can be seen as a way of shaping expected behaviour and appropriate ways of being in rural landscapes. As Guida noted, boisterous singing was tied up with conversations in the press, and amongst more traditional middle-class walking groups, around who were 'true ramblers' and what kind of behaviour was deemed appropriate to truly appreciate being in nature.[212] For instance, Ward made a strong distinction between ramblers and hikers, dedicating a short article to this topic in the 1951–52 SCR handbook in which he described the best use of the term 'hiker' 'is to apply it to our now young parasites, hangers on or spongers' and 'the wilful damage-doers'.[213] Elsewhere, he described the hiker as 'little less than town nuisance wherever he goes' and 'almost as great a danger to general "Access to Mountains" as the medievally-minded moor-owner'.[214] Here, the inappropriate behaviour of those who were outside the rambling fraternity were seen as not just disruptive but potentially having a negative impact on the aims of many outdoor recreation organisations in campaigning for greater access to the countryside. There is also a paternalistic overtone of desiring to shape and manage the behaviour of urban working-classes as a means of improvement for themselves and society as a whole, as previously mentioned in Section 2. Ward argued that people 'lack education in the art of spending their leisure time' and that 'a rambler made was a man improved' (see Figure 6).[215]

Within the scouting movement, singing was framed as part of the movement's aim to 'improve on the dullness and artificiality of modern life' through

---

[211] Alan Mattingly, 'Viewpoint', *CHA Magazine*, 74: 1 (Summer 1980), 5–7, p. 7.
[212] Guida, *Listening to British Nature*.
[213] George H. B. Ward, 'The Rambler and "Hiker"', *Sheffield Clarion Ramblers Handbook 1951–52*: 67–70, p. 69.
[214] Ward, 'Three Men of the Moors', p. 83.
[215] George H. B. Ward, 'Ramblers all: Zest, Health and Joy', *Sheffield Clarion Ramblers Handbook 1921–22*: 58–61, pp. 60–61.

Figure 6 Cover of the *Sheffield Clarion Ramblers Handbook 1925–26*, featuring a photograph of a man standing atop a cairn with his fist held in the air. The tagline on the cover reads 'A rambler made is a man improved'. Credit: Sheffield Local Studies Library.

providing scouts and guides the opportunity to experience and create beauty and develop the artistic part of their nature.[216] One of Leonard's drivers for founding

---

[216] Barclay, *Campfire Singing for Scouts and Guides*, p. 9.

the CHA was a perception that 'people – more particularly those who worked in the Lancashire Mills – needed to learn how to spend their holidays'.[217] Writing specifically about the CHA, but with a sentiment that can be applied to many of the outdoor recreation groups of this period, Snape has argued:

> The type of leisure promoted was thus grounded upon a rejection of materialism, conspicuous consumption and rowdy behaviour, in favour of simplicity, affordability and a sober, interpretative and quiet enjoyment of the countryside that later provided a foundation for the unwritten behavioural codes of countryside leisure practice.[218]

Elements of these behavioural codes would of course eventually be written down and targeted at recreational (and often urban) users of rural spaces by organisations such as the Ramblers Association, the Open Spaces Society, the Council for the Preservation of Rural England, and consolidated in a national Country Code, launched in 1951.[219] However, what we can see in groups such as the SCR and CHA is the translation of ideas of countryside citizenship at a smaller scale – within the specific communities of their groups.

The CHA aimed to offer an alternative to what Leonard perceived as the 'demoralising influence' of 'inane and trivial' holidays spent at seaside resorts like Blackpool, which were portrayed as unhealthily overcrowded, costly, and lacking 'any rational idea of enjoyment'.[220] However, he did not want this to be 'at the expense of bringing the Blackpool spirit and Blackpool noise into the countryside'.[221] Similarly, Ward wrote that 'good ramblers select a better place for their summer holidays' than Blackpool, and also railed against 'Butlinism'.[222] Open-air singing played a role in these debates both in terms of the songs chosen and the way they were sung.

In December 1910, Leonard wrote in *Comradeship* about the rise of a level of exuberance amongst members which was, for him at least, at odds with the ethos of the CHA and responsible ways of being in the countryside. The ensuing debate illustrated the challenges in striking a balance between a desirable level of enthusiasm for collective singing and undesirable 'rowdiness'. The link to ideas of appropriate citizenship here was made explicit as he described the 'singing and

---

[217] Gregory, 'T.A. Leonard', p. 643.
[218] Snape, 'The Co-operative Holidays Association and the Cultural Formation of Countryside Leisure Practice', p. 156.
[219] Gavin Parker, 'The Country Code and the Ordering of Countryside Citizenship', *Journal of Rural Studies*, 22 (2006), 1–16. Interestingly, it is not until the 1982 iteration of the code that reference to noise is included.
[220] Gregory, 'T.A. Leonard', p. 643, and Taylor, *A Claim on the Countryside*, p. 203.
[221] Leonard, 'To Our Members', *Comradeship*, 4:3 (December 1910), 35–36, p. 36.
[222] George H. B. Ward, 'Brazen Blackpool', *Sheffield Clarion Ramblers Handbook 1954–55*, 68–69, p. 69, and Ward, 'Three Men of the Moors', p. 84.

rocketting' at railway stations as 'unmannerly' and complained of 'the uncontrolled way we let ourselves go on mountain tops and other quiet sanctuaries of natural beauty, to our own loss and to the unspeakable annoyance of strangers who may be there'. He saw this as a new development in the movement:

> It seems as if we were getting into a rowdy way of singing songs. At certain centres, last summer, during certain weeks, hardly anything but the noisiest, rollicking songs were ever sung, and Macnamara's Band was yelled morning, noon and night, indoors and out, among the silent hills by day, and along country lanes at night, to the exasperation of quiet folk, until all but the noise-lovers were tired out.[223]

This can be read as an early example of concerns around bringing undesirable elements of urban-life into rural settings, which were epitomised in debates around the hiking craze of the 1920s and 1930s and were seen to detract from the benefits and freedoms that rational and moral enjoyment through rambling could bring.[224] The modern songs chosen and the rowdy way in which they were sung reflected ways of being in the landscape perceived by some members of rambling groups as inappropriate. For instance, the historian Ben Anderson has cited extracts from 1931 Manchester Ramblers' Federation's Rambler's Handbook, in which Edwin Royce complained of hikers 'hanging in ape-like festoons on (apparently) precipitous crags moaning – with ukelele distractions – the latest banality in the approved whining tenor style'.[225] The language used and the characterisation of inappropriate behaviour as animalistic here underlines the portrayal as this kind of behaviour as uncivilised. Boddice and Smith have also highlighted this, writing about Smithfield Market in the nineteenth century, as a 'moral re-framing' of behaviour set in the context of ideas of what constitutes a civilised society, which extended to a desire to control the sensory elements of behaviour 'including the production of smells, sounds and sights, in public and commercial spaces'.[226] In our context, the public space is the rural leisure landscape of the hillside, path and trail.

We can also see, in these examples, the employment of sound, including singing, as a way to distinguish between ramblers (as a specific form of open-air enthusiast and citizen) and other visitors from towns. Inappropriate behaviour is depicted as detrimental to all involved: to the 'true' ramblers who may be incorrectly associated with their rowdy counterparts, to the people who live and work in the countryside and to the misbehaving persons themselves who miss out on the potential benefits of being in the open air. The urban-ness of these

---

[223] Leonard, 'To Our Members', p. 36.
[224] Ben Anderson, 'A Liberal Countryside? The Manchester Ramblers' Federation and the "Social Readjustment" of Urban Citizens, 1929–1936', *Urban History* 38: 1 (2011), 84–102.
[225] *Ibid.*, p. 14.   [226] Boddice and Smith, *Emotion, Sense, Experience*, p. 11.

visitors is characterised as preventing them from perceiving and appreciating sensory aspects of the rural environment: 'Their ears are closed to the numerous calls borne across the country air and their eyes see but very little of the country they traverse, simply because, mentally, they have not left the town at all.'[227]

It is no surprise that the instrument brought along by these rowdier visitors (and criticised in ramblers' publications) is the ukulele – emblematic of the music hall and cinematic entertainments of the town. Again, we see here the positioning of behaviour and music associated with urban life as out of place and inappropriate within the open-air movement. This is set in stark contrast to the 'unobtrusive' and 'thoughtful' rambler who 'adjusts himself as far as possible to the countryman's world ... the idea of carrying the noisy atmosphere of the town into country places is repugnant to him'.[228] Even subtle signs of urban backgrounds such as the 'nasal twang' when singing, which was observed as a 'habit, especially with Town scouts', were to be gently mocked and corrected by leaders within the scouting movement.[229]

However, within the co-operative holiday movement at least, deciding at which point open-air singing went from being enthusiastic to inappropriate was neither straightforward nor an objective matter. In December 1912, a CHA member wrote in defence of 'the hilarity and breeziness that should be the possession of noble-minded youth' – which was not to be confused with 'uncontrolled rowdyism' – and admonished the association for being too restrictive and authoritarian in its expectations of ways of being in the countryside:

> It is scarcely fair that we who wish to be natural should be repressed when we start some rollicking song on a breezy moorland walk or after having successfully conquered some mountain summit, such as Cader Idris.[230]

For this member, singing as part of outdoor recreation was one of the few ways he could be himself and enjoy a level of freedom and personal autonomy not experienced in his urban, working life:

> For fifty weeks in the year we often have to supress any personal views and ideas we have just because we realise that our employers have the power of taking our bread and butter away from us.[231]

It is possible that open-air singing provided a valued outlet for expression of both self and emotions for these young people. Certainly 'breaking into song

---

[227] Harold E. Wild, 'The Unobtrusive Rambler', in Manchester Ramblers' Federation, *The Rambler's Handbook 1928*, 29–30, p. 30.
[228] *Ibid.*   [229] Barclay, *Campfire Singing for Scouts and Guides*, p. 13.
[230] H. T., 'The C.H.A.: A Criticism', *Comradeship*, 6: 3 (December 1912), 35–36, p. 35.
[231] *Ibid.*

may be a sign of emotion'.[232] As Steven Graham asked, 'what is a tramping day if it does not liberate a voice, so that you can sing out your soul to the free sky'.[233] Feld has noted that sensory experiences in the present can evoke emotions and recall past experiences and through this connection of 'ear and heart' with a 'lost repertoire of music' a sense of freedom is regained.[234] In a similar vein, Steven Graham reflected that songs which came to mind and voice whilst walking were often 'something remembered from childhood and school days':

> 'Sing me a song of a lad that is gone' – it is singing that song over and over again on never-tiring ears. 'Say, could that lad be I?' – it is asking the question, and your light heart is answering, 'Yes, yes, that lad was I. The tiresome somber fellow who worked in a town was not I. I was imprisoned in him. Now I am free and I sing'.[235]

Could the act of collective, enthusiastic singing, alongside strenuous rambles, be seen as a way of channelling the exuberant energy of youth in what was deemed to be healthy and acceptable ways as well as reconnecting with the innocent freedom of childhood? Certainly, J. L. Paton suggested it was 'the fun there is in altogetherness' that was at the heart of the founding of the CHA, and that this fun could be 'noisy', 'the explosive sort'.[236] Walford-Davies, too, suggested that singing could also be an outlet and balm for the anxieties of a generation during wartime: 'a good songbook is like a bosom friend because it responds to many phases of ourselves, and gives timely relief to the varied feelings it expresses' and 'there was never a time when song was more needed than today'.[237]

As we have seen, the experience of escape and freedom from the rigours of industrial and urban working lives were an important part of the ethos of outdoor recreation groups at this time. However, there were limits counselled on the appropriate expression of this freedom. Just as there were respectable expectations of the behaviour of mixed groups of men and women on CHA holidays, which frowned upon 'familiarities' such as rambling with linked arms or resting one's head in another's lap – 'of which ashamed C.H.A. friends (real jolly holiday folk of the right sort) occasionally tell!' – so were there attempts to constrain and shape the way people expressed themselves through song.[238] As the author of another letter in *Comradeship* in 1912 highlighted 'shouting of songs on a mountain top is a natural expression of elation to one group, it

---

[232] Rosenwein, *Generations of Feeling*, p. 4.
[233] Graham, *The Gentle Art of Tramping*, p. 132.   [234] Feld, 'Waterfalls of Song', p. 92.
[235] Graham, *The Gentle Art of Tramping*, pp. 129–130.
[236] J. L. Paton, 'At Our Annual Meeting', *Comradeship*, 29: 3 (Spring 1938), p. 8.
[237] Walford-Davies, 'Our New Songbook', pp. 9–10.   [238] Leonard, 'To Our Members', p. 35.

absolutely spoils the enjoyment of another'.[239] One way that this was addressed was through guidance around how to approach group singing. The combined CHA and HF songbook, *Songs of Faith, Nature and Fellowship,* gave detailed seven-point instructions around how best to learn and sing new songs, with point four advising 'don't be afraid of trying the slower and quieter songs. These form a pleasant relief from the "hullabaloo" style'.[240] Similarly, advice for open-air singing within the scouting movement cautioned that 'shouting must be absolutely taboo, even in jolly choruses'.[241]

Further comments by Leonard in the pages of *Comradeship* highlighted tensions between 'the rollicking good humour and high spirit of our Guest Houses, which is the natural outcome of healthy exercise, stimulating companionship, an abundance of fresh air and sunshine' (which was welcomed) and a minority of guests who indulged 'in midnight parades with singing and accessories, which are not always, we fear, spontaneous outbursts of fun, but a sort of hollow and objectionable ritual'.[242] For the CHA these behaviours were enough to ban some offenders from holiday centres. These letters clearly speak to a tension within the movement, which itself reflected wider conflict between different groups enjoying the countryside in different ways, and for whom singing was part of the outward expression of identity and emotion. Returning to notions of fellow-feeling discussed in section two, this was not only a process of negotiating ways of being in the countryside but of challenging the norms within the community of the CHA itself, and perhaps of tension between different 'generations of feeling' within the emotional community of the co-operative holiday movement.[243] As Edith Turner has noted:

> Communitas is exciting; it makes people able to organize and work together. With this power, they will eventually develop organizational habits, structures, and rules of behavior, and ranks and positions. These often work well, if they remain on the human level; yet if they become overly law-bound, communitas will bubble up again from below and question the old system.[244]

Although Ward also wrote against the rowdy behaviour of some Peak District visitors, he tended to define this in terms of physical violence and vandalism.[245]

---

[239] F. P., 'A Reply', *Comradeship*, 6: 3 (December 1912), 36–36, p. 36.
[240] The CHA and HF, *Songs of Faith, Nature and Fellowship,* foreword (no page number).
[241] Barclay, *Campfire Singing for Scouts and Guides*, p. 13.
[242] T. A. Leonard, 'Conduct and Commonsense', *Comradeship*, 6:5 (April 1913), 66–67, p. 67.
[243] Rosenwein, *Generations of Feeling.*   [244] Turner, *Communitas*, p. 4.
[245] G. H. B. Ward, 'Vandalism in paradise', *Sheffield Clarion Ramblers Handbook 1950–51*, 176–179.

In his foreword for the SCR songbook, he appears to take a more inclusive approach to enthusiastic singing outdoors: 'let us raise our voices that their echoes may resound from Pendle Hill to Kinderscout'.[246] He did, however, complain about loud singing of 'dance songs' and playing of 'instruments' on the platforms of railway stations in rural locations, arguing this represented 'silliness in public places'.[247]

In the context of these debates, the publication of appropriate songs to sing in the countryside through the various songbooks from outdoor recreation groups could be seen as another way of shaping and regulating ways of being in the landscape. For instance, Sarah Mills has noted that many of the songs included in the Woodcraft folk's songbooks 'were incredibly self-affirming and drew most powerfully on distinctions between idealised rural landscapes and the (im)moral landscape of the city'.[248] As such, they were part socialisation and articulation of the model of citizenship that young people within the movement were encouraged to embody. Certainly, Ward saw that the socialisation of youth through rambling clubs was a means to address the issue of 'vandalism in paradise'.[249] With regard to rowdyism, he urged 'action to prevent thoughtless behaviour in the countryside rather than keeping people out' and highlighted the role of singing in this too: 'Let us not have one rambling club but fifty, and a song on every journey and light hearts to the end.'[250] Similarly, Anderson has described how the Manchester Ramblers' Federation sought to 'persuade rather than force "hikers" into becoming "ramblers"' through education (signage, handbooks and talks) and guided experience (from volunteer Warden-Guides in the landscape).[251]

In shaping townsfolk into the rambling model of moral outdoor citizenship, these groups aimed to influence people's character and ways of being beyond the time they spent in rural environments, with the implication that they would take this behaviour back into their lives in urban centres. In Ward's song 'A Mountain Thought' he wrote:

> That mountains make men strong and great,
> Prepared to stand but not to lean;
> To change the false, exalt the true,
> And make the city sweet and clean.[252]

---

[246] Ward, *Songs for Ramblers to Sing on the Moorlands*, p. 1.
[247] Anon, 'Silliness in public places', *Sheffield Clarion Ramblers Handbook 1928–29*, p. 144.
[248] Mills, '"A powerful educational instrument"', p. 71.
[249] Ward, 'Vandalism in paradise', p. 176.
[250] Holt, *G.H.B. Ward 1876–1957*, p. 1, and Ward, 'Ramblers all', p. 60.
[251] Ben Anderson, 'A liberal countryside? The Manchester Ramblers' Federation and the "social readjustment" of urban citizens, 1929–1936', *Urban History* 38:1 (2011), 84–102, p. 97.
[252] Ward, *Songs for Ramblers to Sing on the Moorlands*, p. 4.

3.3 Place Connections and Connectedness

It is not just singing in rural landscapes that builds meanings of and connections with place but the type and lyrics of songs play a role here too. The HF introduced a 1929 edition of *Songs by the Way* with the following advice:

> It is hoped that due care will be exercised in the choosing of songs for outdoor use. A song that is adapted to the more artificial conditions within walls may be quite out of place within natural conditions.[253]

Ward outlined in the foreword to the SCR songbook how he favoured English folk songs as they had 'the very breath of the countryside in its jingling rhymes'.[254] The late nineteenth and early twentieth centuries saw the emergence of two entangled movements one focused on outdoor recreation and access to the countryside led by a range of local and national groups, the other a revival of interest in folk-song led by high profile collectors such as Cecil Sharp.[255] For some these reflected contemporary Romantic and anti-modernity discourses that positioned the rural as central to English identity and heritage.[256] Commenting on the proliferation of organisations set up in the late nineteenth century to preserve and protect aspects of nature, heritage and landscape, Charles Frake has noted:

> we can see something very 'English' in this joint concern with such things as plants, animals, footpaths, natural beauty, ancient monuments and old buildings – all to be protected and preserved, not so much 'as they are' but rather 'as they were' in an imagined past of pleasant places.[257]

Thus singing folk songs whilst in the landscape could be seen as one way people connected with a perceived heritage of the countryside, and a nostalgia for an imagined ideal of English rural life. In this way the connectedness is with an ideal, rather than real, place. It is a connection with an idea of the countryside – a perhaps very white, middle-class, male (and anti-modernity) perspective – rather than an engagement with the countryside as it actually was at the time: as a living, working and in many ways modern and industrialised landscape.

---

[253] The Holiday Fellowship, *Fellowship Holidays*, p. 2.
[254] Ward, *Songs for Ramblers to Sing on the Moorlands*, p. 1.
[255] See Taylor, *A Claim on the Countryside*, for more on campaigns for access to the countryside and the growth of outdoor recreation movements.
[256] See Matless, *Landscape and Englishness,* and Paul Readman, *Storied Ground: Landscape and the Shaping of English National Identity* (Cambridge: Cambridge University Press, 2018), for more on this topic.
[257] Charles O. Frake, 'Pleasant places, past times, and sheltered identity in rural East Anglia', in S. Feld and K. Basso (eds) *Senses of Place* (Santa Fe: School of American Research Press, 2011), 229–257, pp. 229–230.

We can also see a tailoring of songs to the local landscapes known to outdoor recreation groups. For example, many of the parodies and re-written club songs from groups such as the SCR and Rucksack Club referenced local places frequented by ramblers and climbers. In the SCR songbook there are songs describing the joys of being on moorlands in all weathers, and what appears to have been the club's signature song 'Land of Moor and Heather' is a rewrite of 'Land of Hope and Glory', with a chorus that celebrates a love for 'Derbyshire the free!' Other songs mention specific places (villages, public houses and landscape features) within Derbyshire and the local countryside. These would have been well-known to regular ramblers within the group. Sometimes, the places mentioned were further afield (such as Helvellyn and Crib Goch) but still connected to group experiences of these places, for example, through recalling club holidays and rambles in the Lake District and North Wales respectively. Even in the songbooks of nationally focused organisations, there are songs dedicated to specific places (e.g. 'Richmond Park' and 'The South Country' in the scouting movement's songbook).[258] We can imagine that these songs enabled those that had rambled in these landscapes to express and cement their personal and group connection with these places. For those that had not experienced these places directly, the songs offered a way of knowing them set in the context of the group community and culture.

In SCR songs the home-grown lyrics don't just express a love for and connection with the local moorlands, but also have a political angle. Many bemoan the lack of access to these landscapes, encourage trespass and point out the injustices of the current state of land ownership. They look to a future where through determined and collective action the northern moorlands are opened up for free and easy access for people from local urban centres. For instance, 'We're Twenty-One Today', with new words written by W. H. Whitney, included the lines:

> We're here to keep our mountain paths,
> We're out to free the moor.
> The moorland is our birthright,
> And the fight will not be won
> Until our native soil belongs
> To every mother's son.[259]

Published more than two decades before the 1949 National Parks and Access to the Countryside Act, one can imagine how evocative it may have been to sing these songs on SCR rambles along the limited public footpaths, in full view of

---

[258] Poyser, *The Open Air Songbook*, p. 57 and p. 129.
[259] Ward, *Songs for Ramblers to Sing on the Moorlands*, p. 20.

open moorland where there was, as-yet, little public access. Singing has often been part of collective place-based activism associated with historical campaigns for greater public access to the countryside. For instance, socialist songs were sung on both the Kinder and Abbey Brook trespasses in 1932.[260]

In this section we have explored how singing in rural landscape was both a way of developing and expressing the meaning that these places held for the people who spent time within them. We have also seen how singing was part of articulating and shaping expectations of appropriate ways of being in the countryside, often set in contrast with modern urban life. However, where, how and what people sung could also challenge these, sometimes restrictive, expectations and be a provocative act – expressing strong emotions, desires for freedom and political aspirations.

Until now we have focused mainly on the historical material, where some aspects of the meaning and emotions form personal experience of communal singing in the open-air may not be readily accessible from analysis of archival sources. In the next section, we bring our research into the present day by discussing the resonances and dissonances with the past via present-day interview data collected using go-along methods and looking forward to how this approach can open up research areas for other scholars and ask wider questions about the ways in which we relate to places using sound and the body.

4 Contemporary Connections and Resonances

Singing continued to be part of Co-operative Holiday Association (CHA) activities into the late twentieth century but it's unclear to what extent this included collective singing outdoors.[261] For instance, an article in *Comradeship* from 1948 described a successful music themed 'cultural week' at their Fullaton House holiday centre and its almost transformational impact on fellow-feeling: 'The common bond of Music welded us together in a manner which had to be experienced to be believed.'[262] However, the foreword to the combined CHA and HF songbook (1951) also noted that 'communal singing at our centres is not quite so popular as it used to be'.[253] By 1966, the General Secretary's address, 'A contemporary holiday association', articulated the CHA's need to move with the times, away from compulsory and prescriptive activities, asking, 'why should we make them conform?' They encouraged the CHA to reflect societal changes and adjust their offer to appeal to a contemporary populace who are

---

[260] Keith Warrender, *Forbidden Kinder: The 1932 Mass Trespass Re-visited* (Timperley: Willow, 2022).
[261] Hope, 'The democratisation of tourism in the English Lake District'.
[262] J. A. Stimpson, 'Musical memories of Totnes', *Comradeship*, 40: 2 (Winter 1948), p. 3.
[263] The CHA and HF, *Songs of Faith, Nature and Fellowship,* Foreword (no page number).

'much more impressed by modernity'.[264] These societal changes included a shift towards spending outdoor leisure time in smaller/family groups, made possible in part by the rise of car-ownership. This contrasted with the collective forms of public transport largely used by early twentieth-century ramblers and holiday-makers, and the dormitory-style accommodation in CHA and HF centres.

The smaller role played by collective singing may also have been influenced by the growing popularity of music playing devices. In 1960, a piece in *CHA Magazine* called for specialist volunteers 'to give particular attention to problems arising in connection with gramophones and gramophone records'.[265] This may have reflected a shift away from collective singing toward listening to recorded music with different implications for indoor and open-air musical enjoyment. As we have already seen, music-playing devices such as gramophones and transistor radios were being taken out into the landscape and had been the focus of complaints in the publications of some rambling groups and the CHA, indicating they were perceived very differently to communal singing outdoors.

Although collective singing may have been less popular as a formal activity, informally people may have continued their open-air singing practices. For example, whilst a Clarion Group, interviewed for an oral history project in 2012, suggested that the group singing on SCR rambles did not continue after Ward's death in 1957, another interviewee (Bill Emmingham) described carrying on what he framed as 'traditions' individually, singing or reading from an old Woodcraft Folk songbook after stopping for lunch on a walk.[266] This suggests that singing, even without the co-ordination of key figures like Ward, was still a part of individual practice, although others suggest that group practices also continued in various ways. Bill Dodds, who attended an event we ran on the historical songbooks as part of the 2023 national Being Human festival at the Northern Stage, Newcastle, remembered that from 1982 to 1998 he helped to organise a monthly ramble from his workplace:

> There were usually 12–15 of us and we used to hire a coach to take us to the Yorkshire Dales, Lake District, Southern Scotland etc for day walks. We always ended up singing when we were on the move or whilst sitting on the grass having lunch breaks. Singing invariably continued in the pub and on the bus home. The type of songs we sang included This Land Is Your Land

---

[264] Mr Wright, 'A contemporary holiday association', *CHA Magazine*, 57: 1 (Summer 1966), 5–7, p. 6.
[265] Anon, 'C.H.A. specialists', *CHA Magazine*, 52: 1 (Summer 1960), p. 22.
[266] Transcripts of interviews with Clarion Group and Bill Emmingham, in Moors for the Future, *Moor Memories*.

(Woody Guthrie), Botany Bay (Trad), Leaving Of Liverpool (Trad), Manchester Rambler (Ewan McColl) etc etc. Singing songs together certainly added to our enjoyment of walking in scenic places and often helped overcome any tiredness. Singing also helped forge a much closer link between group members.[267]

Dodds notes that after 1998 even though the monthly walks continued the singing element started to die out. This may have been a particular change related to that group but it does suggest that singing itself in this format continued throughout the twentieth century.

Beyond the historic groups we have been discussing there are many contemporary groups and individuals for whom group singing continues to be part of their embodied and sensorial engagements with the countryside. For some there is a political aspect to their singing, linked to campaigns for access to rural landscapes. Commoners Choir is 'an active, contemporary political choir' based in Leeds, which incorporates outdoor performance as part of their practice and 'conceives both singing and walking as political acts of protest and commemoration' connecting with an historical context of singing as a way to challenge and critique inequality going back to the fourteenth century, and of performing these songs in places where they will have an impact.[268] Other groups combine interests and practices of singing outdoors as part of leisure activities, such as the natural voice choirs Wild Chorus and Lakeland Voice.[269] It is to these contemporary practices that we now turn our attention, to explore the connections and resonances between open-air singing practices of both the past and the present.

For our discussion of open-air singing in the early and mid-twentieth century, we have drawn on published sources, which were written away from the direct experience of singing in the open air. These were often produced by the organisers of outdoor recreation groups rather than by ordinary members and participants. In contrast, our contemporary data comes from interviews with members of an open-air singing group, conducted whilst they were out singing and walking in the landscape. These two sources of data come from very different social and cultural contexts. By including this present-day perspective, we are not suggesting that the perspectives of open-air singers today are

---

[267] From email correspondence to Abbi Flint post event on 22 November 2023 with permission to cite in publications given.

[268] Lisa Taylor and Boff Whalley, '"Real change comes from below!": Walking and singing about places that matter; the formation of Commoners Choir', *Leisure Studies*, 38: 1 (2019), 58–73, p. 58.

[269] More on Wild Chorus here www.mouthfulway.co.uk/wild and on Lakeland Voice here https://lakelandvoice.co.uk/.

analogous to the experiences and views of those in the past. As we hope to have made clear in the preceding sections, the experiences of singing and being in rural landscapes in the past were influenced by complex, situated factors, including but not limited to the social and political context of the time, discourses around nature, citizenship and health, and the lived experiences of the people involved. What we do propose is that by exploring open-air singing using multiple methods, in our case archival research and go-along interviews, we can explore different facets of the experience and meaning of open-air singing for those who led and participated in it, and through that open up potential avenues for future study.

4.1 'Greater than the Sum of Its Parts'

Our case study of present-day open-air singing is drawn from a go-along interview with a singing group (Lakeland Voice) who incorporate walking in suburban and rural landscapes within their practice in the summer months of June and July, as well as singing and walking trips away.[270] Their singing walks typically took place in the evening, covered about four miles, and included several stops to sing along the way (see Figure 7). Routes were chosen with a number of qualities in mind: the aesthetics, accessibility and suitability of places to sing, and centred on a similar area to our historic groups: the north west of England. With their consent, one of us (Flint) joined the group on one of their scheduled singing walks in July 2023, to experience firsthand what it is like to sing and walk together in the landscape and to speak with members to learn about their experiences.[271]

Below, we explore whether and how these contemporary experiences resonate with historic material, and how these offer an alternative lens through which to enrich our understanding of open-air singing in relation to our three core themes of the body, fellow-feeling, and place.

> Singing can actually be, particularly in parts, I think is a very rewarding activity in and of itself. And walking in the company of friends is also

---

[270] Go-along interviews are an approach within mobile research methods, through which researchers join participants as they move through environments, to explore their experiences and perspectives in situ. For more information see Spinney, 'Close encounters'; Sarah Bell, 'Walking Methods', in Victoria Bates, ed, *Sensory Research in the Humanities: An Introduction to Five Methods* (2023) https://medenvnetwork.wordpress.com/2023/03/28/sensory-research-in-the-humanities/; and, Abbi Flint and Clare Hickman, 'Moving Research: Walking and Other Mobile Methods', in Amber Abrams, Victoria Bates and Rocio Gomez (eds) *Handbook of Health and Environmental Humanities* (Routledge, January 2026). https://research-information.bris.ac.uk/en/publications/the-routledge-handbook-of-health-and-environmental-humanities/.

[271] This part of the research received ethical approval from Newcastle University. With participants consent the interview was recorded and transcribed. The quotations within this section come from the anonymised transcript.

Figure 7 Photograph of members of the Lakeland Voice choir walking. Credit: Abbi Flint.

a pleasant activity. So, to bring the two, bring the two together it's just, it's greater than the sum of its parts I think. (Choir participant).

4.1.1 The Body

The choir started their singing walk with warm-up exercises for both bodies and voices, and the choir leader articulated how singing and walking/being outdoors were seen as complementary, embodied activities:

> The two sort of complement each other ... if I'm with some friends we'll stop and we'll sing – informally. Raising spirits you see ... the two complement each other very nicely – the singing lifts your spirits and the walking opens your lungs up, and engages the body in the singing. (Choir leader).

This quote also picks up on the connection between sociality, singing and emotional feeling, in particular, happiness. The choir leader went on to illustrate the entangled nature of emotions and singing and the difficulty in pinpointing whether one is 'singing because you are happy or are you happy because you are singing'. This was framed as connecting with longer traditions of singing outdoors, particularly associated with physically demanding work (e.g. sailors); 'partly so that they could do fairly boring repetitive work in time but also so that it could lift their spirits in what would otherwise be a probably very unpleasant life'.

In terms of a physical practice, the choir generally stopped walking to sing, but at a couple of points they combined the two. For example, they sang a song about 'swinging along the open road' whilst walking along. There were also connections with notions of resonance, particularly in relation to the physical context of the environment, and the impact this has on the embodied and emotional experience of singing. For instance, noting the different resonances and feelings evoked from singing to an open sky or under cover:

> I think it sometimes can be quite hard when we're singing out in the open like tonight because your voice disappears so you can't as easily hear the other parts. You need to do that to make sure you're harmonising in the same tune . . . erm . . . so it can be, you know, you can easily slip, shall we say . . . so, to have an enclosed area is more successful. So, like under a tree, you know, something like that is more successful. (Choir participant)

Singing in the ruins of buildings and in caves had provided memorable and favourite places to sing, described as 'magical' and 'special'. One participant recalled the distinctive experience and interplay with the other-than-human when singing in a cave (see Figure 8):

> Because of the acoustics . . . You don't have to get it right for it to sound very nice [laughter] and when you stop singing you've still got the sound, obviously reverberates for a while, and then you hear the drip drip drip of the water from the cave. (Choir participant)

As a walking choir the group have had to negotiate encountering livestock, tricky paths in low light or wintry weather, and issues around accessibility and individual mobility. We encountered two stiles which prompted conversation about access difficulties on the singing walk: one a narrow squeeze stile, another a series of steps built into a tall stone wall with no handrail. At another point in the walk, a section of path had slipped into the river requiring a steep step-around. At all these points members of the choir stopped to help one another, offering suggestions of alternative routes, a steadying hand or to hold walking poles whilst people negotiated obstacles. Often accompanied by warmth and humour, these instances reflected the sense of friendship, community and embodied care for one another. One participant spoke of how this sense of care meant she had 'done much more than I thought I could . . . Or I've . . . perhaps something I wouldn't have done. They're very supportive'.

Figure 8 Photograph of Lakeland Voice singing in Rydal Cave in Ambleside. Credit: Alan Cleaver.

4.1.2 Fellow-feeling

The opportunities to socialise in different ways and develop friendships through the shared practices of singing and walking together were valued highly by choir members, and highlighted as something which distinguished this group from other (indoor-only) choirs:

> I think one of the things I've always enjoyed about these sort of trips out is that it's an opportunity to get to know the other people in the choir better. Because when you're singing indoors, you tend to stand in your parts and you don't really get to know the people you don't stand quite close to. And walking and chatting and stopping for a song, it's just a pleasant thing to do really. (Choir participant).
>
> It's just wonderful friendships ... Especially the walks, the walks they're sort of the icing on the cake almost ... because you get to know people much more. (Choir participant)

The choir were a tight-knit group – as one member explained, the core-membership had been part of the choir for so long, and they had such a strong sense of community, that it could make it feel 'quite difficult for new people to come'. However, this did not prevent them forging connections with others when singing outdoors. For example, they described singing in a street choir festival with over 1000 others, which involved a rainy walk to sing in Cathedral Cave, Little Langdale, with a group of around sixty people. This showed that, although a distinctive group in their own right, they saw themselves as part of the wider choir community, suggesting that fellow-feeling in open-air singing may be expressed at multiple levels. These connections were sometimes unexpected and emerged through their open-air singing practices, as this story about a trip overseas revealed:

> We were in the sort of foothills of Triglav, national park, and we stopped by a river and started to sing and some other walkers came along and they stopped to listen to us, they were Slovenian, we chatted to them and it turns out they were part of a choir and ... the following two times in Slovenia we've ended up singing with that choir ... Which could well never have happened if not for the fact that they happened upon us in the national park and realised we were a choir because we were singing. If we hadn't been singing you see we'd just have been another group of walkers. (Choir participant)

Here we can see how open-air singing marked the choir out as distinctive, not simply another walking group. This distinctiveness, in conjunction with the opportunity to meet like-minded people, was a factor that drew people to join the choir; it held an element of novelty that piqued people's interest.

> it was the walking singing that drew me, yes ... it had the two things I love doing [laughter] linked together really. (Choir participant)

As well as a locus of sociality, open-air singing was also an enriching individual experience, often intersecting with participants' sense of identity and personal life history. There was a sense that the combination of singing and walking and being in the open-air took the pressure off the performance aspects of singing together.

4.1.3 Place and the Other-than-Human

Singing whilst walking brought the choir into connection and conversation with other-than-human aspects of environments. For instance, the choir leader spoke of how singing outdoors was 'enhancing the natural beauty of the landscape'. These connections became entangled with the choir's practices and influenced their experiences in multi-sensory ways. During the go-along interview, birds sang in the background, the sounds of the river and wind were present, dogs barked, and ducks quacked. Participants mentioned wildlife as we encountered it, including flowers, trees, birds and insects. However, the other-than-human was not always perceived positively or as 'natural'. The walk took us past a water treatment works which one participant described as an 'overpowering stench'. As we walked together the sounds of traffic and industry, music from car stereos, alongside the voices of people humming, singing, whistling and talking, accompanied us at points. These were not always felt to be in harmony (quite literally) with open-air singing – for instance participants remarked on how sounds from distant traffic caused them to lose their key:

> Choir leader: There was something on a different note over there. I think it was some body's brakes in b flat.
> Participant: I think it's the trains.

Similarly, one participant recalled the reaction of cattle to the choir singing in a working agricultural landscape as unpredictable, humorous but also possibly dangerous. The participant had worried the cows would 'get spooked' as they 'didn't look very happy', but

> They'd listened to one song, when we started the second song, they just turned tail and bolted away from us! And it was so funny [laughs] because I'd been thinking, you know, we need to be careful with these ... but they were more worried about us! (Choir participant)

Choices of what and where to sing were also in conversation with the environment. For instance, when the group encountered swifts and sand-martins along a stretch of the river, the choir leader introduced a new round to sing: 'Here's a bird song [sings] – Ah, poor bird, wing thy flight, high above the sorrows of this dark night.' There was a joyful spontaneity to this practice – decisions about where they paused to sing and what they sang happened on the hoof, often shaped by encounters with human and other-than-human actors in the landscape. By an open stretch of river, they stopped to sing a river related song, and paused under a lime tree to sing a Slovenian song about the tree which wove in themes of seasonality, loss and hope. As with the historical singing practices we have explored, we can see here a feeling of connection between the singers and aspects of the other-than-human environment (birds, trees, rivers) expressed and articulated through song. These decisions about where to sing suggest an engagement with place, and of making new connections with place through singing, forging shared memories of 'all the nice places that we've been and sung in'.

4.2 Reflections and Resonances

The relationship between walking and singing is very different in our contemporary case study compared with our historical groups. Whereas the SCR, CHA and HF were outdoor recreational groups who drew singing into their activities, the walking choir began as an indoor choir, and incorporated walking into their practice after the choir leader experienced 'a choir singing outside the mountain refuge singing, singing to the night as the moon was rising' on an overseas walking holiday. However, there are parallels here with Leonard's inspiration for singing on CHA rambles which, as Douglas Hope described, were influenced by his own experiences of people singing whilst rambling when he spent time in Germany.[272] The choir leader also connected the choir's practice with historical traditions of singing outdoors in both leisure and work, including by sailors and ramblers.

This Element has focused on the interplay between body, feelings and place when singing in the open air. In contrast to the archival material, the exploration of a contemporary walking choir, in situ through a go-along interview, enabled us to probe more deeply into the individual as well as the collective experience of group singing, and the complex motivations, emotions and aspects of self and memories these involve. Through this we can see common threads across historical and present-day experiences in terms of the capacity for collective, open-air singing to inspire fellow-feeling and community, and that singing outdoors can forge memorable connections with place. Although the composition of co-created soundscapes in the past and present were very different, we also get a sense that in each there are natural elements which are welcomed and in harmony with group singing (e.g. bird song and the sound of rivers), and elements more associated with town and industry which are perceived less positively (such as the sound of traffic and trains in the present, and the sound of transistor radios and motorbikes in the past). Reflecting on insights from the go-along interview also prompts questions for potential future studies. For instance, how were decisions about what and where to sing made by outdoor groups in the past? What was the balance between singing whilst moving and when stopped in the landscape? And, how might the notion of 'care' be a fruitful lens for exploring connections between fellow-feeling amongst members of groups and the environments they spent time in and how this linked to place-connectedness?

In this Element, we have focused on open-air singing in the context of outdoor leisure on foot, but the thematic focus on the body, senses, feelings and place can apply to a wide range of other open-air singing contexts. As part of the In All Our Footsteps project we ran two public engagement events sharing our research into open-air singing in the early twentieth century, and audience members generously shared their own experiences of singing. Their experiences spoke to a huge diversity of group and individual practices which included singing outdoors on boats and quaysides, whilst cycling, on political marches, whilst camping, at festivals, in voluntary working groups, in parks and on allotments. Clearly, this is a practice that resonates in the present and still has

---

[272] Hope, *Whatever Happened to 'Rational' Holidays for Working People c.1919–2000?*

value and meaning for people today and there is much scope for further study of these varied open-air singing contexts.

4.3 Conclusion

Our discussion of the connections between singing and place, and ideas of appropriate behaviours and ways of being in the countryside, illustrates the importance of understanding the social and cultural context of emotional and sensory histories. As Coates eloquently writes, 'noise is to sound what stench is to smell (and what weed is to plant)-something dissonant, unwanted, out of place, and invasive. But notions of noise, sound, and silence-like any other cultural phenomena-are invariably historically contingent, varying according to time, place, and human constituency'.[273] Drawing together experiences and accounts of collective outdoor singing from the archive and the present day, we hope to have illustrated the complex, plural and sometimes contradictory ways that singing, sociality, wellbeing and landscape intersect. Singing outdoors can be an expression of connection with one another, with nature and the other-than-human, with memory and identity, and with senses of wellbeing and spirituality. It can also be a political and provocative act; it can serve to build fellow-feeling and include or marginalise and exclude. It can be a free expression of feeling and desire, or a way to shape and channel energy and emotions within normative conceptions of the countryside and outdoor leisure. By understanding the diverse ways in which the human voice, through song, has engaged with being in landscape in the past, we open up potential for more inclusive and multi-sensory approaches to landscape access and engagement in the future.

---

[273] Coates, 'The Strange Stillness of the Past', p. 643.

Bibliography

Alpha of the Plough, 'In praise of walking', in Manchester Ramblers' Federation, *The Rambler's Handbook 1923*. P. 20.

Anderson, Ben, 'A liberal countryside? The Manchester Ramblers' Federation and the "social readjustment" of urban citizens, 1929–1936', *Urban History*, 38: 1 (2011), 84–102.

Anon, *International Tramping Tours Songbook*. Leeds: International Tramping Tours (no date), p. 2.

Anon, 'Pleasures of the countryside', *The Circle*, 1: 9 (1908), p. 217.

Anon, 'A holiday Experience', Comradeship, 5:1 (September 1911), 15–16.

Anon, 'Tunebook', *Comradeship*, 5: 5 (April 1912), p. 67.

Anon, 'Our songbook', *Comradeship*, 8: 2 (December 1914), p. 3.

Anon, 'The Fellowship Songbook', *Comradeship*, 9: 2 (December 1915), p. 11.

Anon, *National Agricultural Labourers' and Rural Workers' Union Songbook*, (Maddermarket, Norwich: Caxton Press, c.1916).

Anon, 'Hints to leaders', *Sheffield Clarion Ramblers Handbook 1919–20*, p. 120.

Anon, 'The 1919 Whitsuntide (climbing) week, – Ambleside Lake District', *Sheffield Clarion Ramblers Handbook 1920–21*, 97–100, p. 100.

Anon, 'Hints to leaders', *Sheffield Clarion Ramblers Handbook 1921–22*, p. 3

Anon, 'Silliness in public places', *Sheffield Clarion Ramblers Handbook 1928–29*, p. 144.

Anon, 'Extracts from our forty-fifth annual report', *Comradeship*, 29: 3 (Spring 1938), 11–14, p. 11.

Anon, 'Access and National Parks', *Sheffield Clarion Ramblers Handbook 1948–49*, p. 130.

Anon, 'Women reveller – ramblers', *Sheffield Clarion Ramblers Handbook 1955–56*, p. 130.

Anon, It's the Derbyshire Air', *Sheffield Clarion Ramblers Handbook 1959–60*, p. 78.

Anon, 'C.H.A. specialists', *CHA Magazine*, 52: 1 (Summer 1960), 22.

Anon, 'Noises off – and on', *Comradeship*, 52: 4 (Winter 1962), p. 27.

Arbuthnot, John, *An Essay Concerning the Effects of Air on Human Bodies* (Printed for J. Tonson in the Strand, 1733), p. vi. Eighteenth Century Collections Online [Accessed 31 January 2025].

Bajwala, Aayushi, 'Walking on the Margin: A Study of Marginalised Ethnic Groups and Their Walking Practices in Urban and Rural Britain', *Field*, 8:1 (2022), 169–186.

Barclay, Kate, 'State of the Field: The History of Emotions', *History*, 106 (2021), 456–466.

Barclay, Vera, ed, *Campfire Singing for Scouts and Guides* (London: Novello, 1934).

Bates, Victoria, *Making Noise in the Modern Hospital, Series: Elements in Histories of Emotions and the Senses* (Cambridge: Cambridge University Press, 2021).

Bell, Phyllis, 'Impressions of a First C.H.A. Holiday', *Comradeship: The Magazine of the Co-operative Holidays Association*, 25 (December 1933), 9–10.

Bell, Sarah, 'Walking Methods', in Victoria Bates, ed, *Sensory Research in the Humanities: An Introduction to Five Methods* (2023) https://medenvnetwork.wordpress.com/2023/03/28/sensory-research-in-the-humanities/.

Bell, Sarah, Hickman, Clare and Houghton, Frank, 'From Therapeutic Landscape to Therapeutic "Sensescape" Experiences with Nature? A Scoping Review', *Wellbeing, Space and Society*, 4 (2022), online: 1–11.

Bender, Barbara, 'Time and Landscape', *Current Anthropology*, 43: S4 (2002), s103–s112.

Benninger, Michael S. and Abitbol, Jean, 'Voice: Dysphonia and the Ageing voice in American Academy of Otolaryngology - Head and Neck Surgery Foundation', *Geriatric Care Otolaryngology* (Alexandria, VA: American Academy of Otolaryngology - Head and Neck Surgery Foundation, 2006), 67–81. https://rlmc.edu.pk/themes/images/gallery/library/books/ENT/Geriatric%20Care%20Otolaryngology.pdf.

Boddice, Rob, *The History of Emotions* (Manchester: Manchester University Press, 2023).

Boddice, Rob and Smith, Mark, *Emotion, Sense, Experience* (Cambridge: Cambridge University Press, 2020).

Byrd, William, *Psalmes, Sonets, & Songs [. . .]* (London: 1599). Via ProQuest. [Accessed 31 January 2025]. https://www.proquest.com/books/psalmes-sonets-songs-sadnes-pietie-made-into/docview/2240852014/se-2 (accessed November 20, 2025).

Camlin, David A., Daffern, Helena and Zeserson, Katherine, 'Group Singing as a Resource for the Development of a Healthy Public', *Humanities and Social Science Communications*, 7: 60 (2020), 1–15.

Bibliography

Casey, Edward S. 'How to Get from Space to Place in a Fairly Short Stretch of Time', in Steven Feld, and Keith H. Basso (eds) *Senses of Place* (Santa Fe: School of American Research Press, 2011), 13–52.

Cloke, Paul, 'Rurality and Racialised Others: Out of Place in the Countryside?' in Neil Chakraborti and Jon Garland, eds, *Rural Racism* (Cullompton: Willan, 2004), 17–35.

Coates, Peter A., 'The Strange Stillness of the Past: Toward an Environmental History of Sound and Noise', *Environmental History*, 10: 4 (2005), 636–665.

Culhane, Dara, 'Sensing', in Denielle Elliott and Dara Culhane, eds, *A Different Kind of Ethnography: Imaginative Practices and Creative Methodologies* (New York: University of Toronto Press, 2017), 45–68.

E. C., 'On Walking', *Sheffield Clarion Ramblers Handbook 1959–60*, 76.

Edensor, Tim, 'Reconnecting with Darkness: Gloomy Landscapes, Lightless Places', *Social & Cultural Geography*, 14: 4 (2013), 446–465. https://doi.org/10.1080/14649365.2013.790992.

Feld, Steven, 'Waterfalls of Song: An Acoustemology of Place Resounding in Bosavi, Papua New Guinea', in Steven Feld and Keith H. Basso, eds, *Senses of Place* (Santa Fe: School of American Research Press, 2011), 91–135.

Flint, Abbi, 'Songs for Ramblers and Songs by the Way: Paths and Trails as Vernacular Contexts for Singing in the Early Twentieth Century', *Folklore*, 136: 3 (2025), 490–515.

Flint, Abbi and Hickman, Clare, 'Moving Research: Walking and Other Mobile Methods', in Amber Abrams, Victoria Bates and Rocio Gomez, eds, *Handbook of Health and Environmental Humanities* (Routledge, January 2026).

F.P., 'A Reply', *Comradeship*, 6: 3 (December 1912), 36–37, p. 36.

Frake, Charles O. 'Pleasant Places, Past Times, and Sheltered Identity in Rural East Anglia', in Steven Feld and Keith H. Basso, eds, *Senses of Place* (Santa Fe: School of American Research Press, 2011), 229–257.

Frixione, Eugenio, 'Pneuma–Fire Interactions in Hippocratic Physiology', *Journal of the History of Medicine and Allied Sciences*, 68: 4 (2013), 505–528.

Gaynor, Andrea, Broomhall, Susan and Flack, Andy, 'Frogs and Feeling Communities: A Study in History of Emotions and Environmental History', *Environment and History*, 28 (2022), 83–104.

Geertz, Clifford, 'Afterword', in Steven Feld and Keith H. Basso (eds) *Senses of Place* (Santa Fe: School of American Research Press, 2011), 259–262.

Goss, John, ed, *'Daily Express' Community Song Book* (London: The London Express Newspaper, 1927).

Graham, Stephen, *The Gentle Art of Tramping* (New York: D. Appleton, 1926).

Gregory, N. H., 'T.A. Leonard: The Pioneer of Fellowship Holidays', *Millgate Monthly*, 36, Part 2: 311 (August 1931), 643–647.

Guida, Michael, *Listening to British Nature: Wartime, Radio, and Modern Life, 1914–1945* (New York: Oxford University Press, 2022).

H. T., 'The C.H.A.: A Criticism', *Comradeship* 6: 3 (December 1912), 35–36, p. 35.

Harker, Ben. '"The Manchester Rambler": Ewan MacColl and the 1932 Mass Trespass', *History Workshop Journal*, 59 (Spring 2005), 219–228. JSTOR, www.jstor.org/stable/25472794.

Henderson, T. 'What Shall I Sing?' *Comradeship*, 7: 5 (May 1914), pp. 69–70.

Hickman, Clare, *Therapeutic Landscapes: A History of English Hospital Gardens since 1800* (Manchester: Manchester University Press, 2013).

Hickman, Clare, 'The Importance of Open Air for Health: Environmental and Medical Intersections', in Tatiana Konrad, ed, *Imagining Air: Cultural Axiology and the Politics of Invisibility* (Exeter: University of Exeter Press, 2023), 180–199.

Hirst, John, ed, *Songs of the Mountaineers* (Manchester: W. Allen Corner, 1922).

Holt, Ann, *G.H.B. Ward 1876–1957: His Lifelong Campaign for Access to the Countryside* (London: The Ramblers' Association, 1985).

Hope, Douglas, *Whatever Happened to 'Rational' Holidays for Working People c.1919–2000? The Competing Demands of Altruism and Commercial Necessity in the Co-operative Holidays Association and Holiday Fellowship*. Doctoral thesis, University of Cumbria (2015).

Hope, Douglas, 'The Democratisation of Tourism in the English Lake District: The Role of the Co-operative Holidays Association and the Holiday Fellowship', *Journal of Tourism History*, 8: 2 (2016), 105–126.

Howes, David, 'The Misperception of the Environment: A Critical Evaluation of the Work of Tim Ingold and an Alternative Guide to the Use of the Senses in Anthropological Theory', *Anthropological Theory*, 22: 4 (2022), 443–466.

Howes, David, *The Sensory Studies Manifesto: Tracking the Sensorial Revolution in the Arts and Human Sciences* (Toronto: University of Toronto Press, 2022).

Ingold, Tim, 'Footprints through the Weather-World: Walking, Breathing, Knowing', *Journal of the Royal Anthropological Institute*, 16: 1 (2010), 121–139.

Ingold, Tim and Vergunst, Jo Lee, 'Introduction', in Tim Ingold and J. L. Vergunst, eds, *Ways of Walking: Ethnography and Practice on Foot* (Farnham: Ashgate, 2008), 1–20.

J. T. G., 'Rapture in the Rain', *Comradeship*, 6:4 (February 1913), p. 64.

Kang, Jing, Scholp, Austin and Jiang, Jack J., 'A Review of the Physiological Effects and Mechanisms of Singing', *Journal of Voice*, 32: 4 (2018), 390–395.

Kayes, Gillyanne, 'Structure and Function of the Singing Voice', in Graham F. Welch, David M. Howard and John Nix, eds, *The Oxford Handbook of Singing*, Oxford Library of Psychology (2019, online ed., Oxford Academic), 3–30.

Knopf, Sigard A., 'Respiratory Exercises in the Prevention and Treatment of Pulmonary Diseases', *Johns Hopkins Medical Bulletin*, 12 (1901), 282–288.

Konrad, Tatiana, ed, *Imagining Air: Cultural Axiology and the Politics of Invisibility* (Exeter: University of Exeter Press, 2023).

Konrad, Tatiana, ed, *Race and Environmental Justice in the Era of Climate Change and COVID-19* (Michigan: Michigan State University Press, 2025).

Leonard, Thomas A., 'To Our Members', *Comradeship*, 4:3, (December 1910), 35–36.

Leonard, Thomas A., 'Conduct and Commonsense', *Comradeship*, 6:5 (April 1913), pp. 66–67.

Leonard, Thomas A. 'Farewell', *Comradeship*, 6:1 (September 1913), p. 4.

Letts, Edmund A., 'The Air We Breathe', in *The Body and Its Health: Being a Course of Lectures Delivered under the Auspices of the Belfast Society for the Extension of University Teaching* (Belfast: Olley, 1892), 67–96. Wellcome Collection. https://wellcomecollection.org/works/v56emh5k.

Luckin, Bill, *Death and Survival in Urban Britain: Disease, Pollution and Environment, 1800–1950* (London: Bloomsbury, 2015).

Masters, David, *How to Conquer Consumption* (London: John Lane, Bodley Head, 1926).

Matless, David, *Landscape and Englishness* (London: Reaktion Books, 2016).

Mattingly, Alan, 'Viewpoint', *CHA Magazine*, 74:1 (Summer 1980), 5–7.

Mills, Sarah, '"A Powerful Educational Instrument": The Woodcraft Folk and Indoor/Outdoor "Nature", 1925–75', in Sarah Mills and Peter Kraftl, eds, *Informal Education, Childhood and Youth* (London: Palgrave Macmillan, 2014), pp. 65–78.

Moors for the Future, *Moor Memories Oral History Project: 'A Living, Working Moorland'. Transcriptions of interviews* (2012). Derbyshire Records Office, D7534.

Morgan-Ellis, Esther M. and Norton, Kay, 'Introduction: Singing as Community, Singing into Community, and Growing the Singing Community', in Esther M. Morgan-Ellis and Kay Norton, eds, *The Oxford Handbook of Community Singing* (Oxford: Oxford University Press, 2024), pp. xxi–xxviii.

Morris, Richard E., 'The Victorian "Change of Air" as Medical and Social Construction,' *Journal of Tourism History*, 10: 1 (2018), 49–65.

Muller, Jørgen Peter, *My Sun-Bathing and Fresh-Air System* (London: Athletic, 1927).

Muthu, David Chowry, *Pulmonary Tuberculosis and Sanatorium Treatment: A Record of 10 Years' Observation and Work in Open-Air Sanatoria* (London: Balliere, Tindall and Cox, 1910).

Muthu, David Chowry, *Pulmonary Tuberculosis: Its Etiology and Treatment. A Record of Twenty Two Years' Observation and Work in Open-Air Sanatoria* (London: Balliere, Tindall and Cox, 1922).

Palmer, Roy, *The Painful Plough* (Cambridge: Cambridge University Press, 1973).

Parker, Gavin, 'The Country Code and the Ordering of Countryside Citizenship', *Journal of Rural Studies*, 22 (2006), 1–16.

Paton, J. L., 'At Our Annual Meeting', *Comradeship*, 29: 3 (Spring 1938), 8–9.

Peak Park Planning Board, *Byelaws for behaviour on access land* (1964). Derbyshire Records Office, D4721/10/1.

Pearce, Georgia, ed, *The Clarion Songbook* (London: The Clarion Press, 1906).

Potter, John and Sorrell, Neil, *A History of Singing* (Cambridge: Cambridge University Press, 2012).

Poyser, Arthur, ed, *The Open Air Songbook* (London: The Boy Scouts Association, 1947).

Prynn, David, 'The Clarion Clubs, Rambling and the Holiday Associations in Britain since the 1890s', *Journal of Contemporary History*, 11 (1976), 65–77.

Readman, Paul, *Storied Ground: Landscape and the Shaping of English National Identity* (Cambridge: Cambridge University Press, 2018).

Revill, George, 'Music and the Politics of Sound: Nationalism, Citizenship, and Auditory Space', *Environment and Planning D: Society and Space*, 18: 5 (2000), 597–613.

Rosenwein, Barbara H., *Generations of Feeling: A History of Emotions, 600–1700* (Cambridge: Cambridge University Press, 2015).

Roud, Steve, *Folk Song in England* (London: Faber and Faber, 2017).

Russell, Dave, 'Abiding Memories: The Community Singing Movement and English Social Life in the 1920s', *Popular Music*, 27: 1 (2008), 117–133.

Russell, Ian, 'Vernacular Christmas Carol Singing in the Southern Pennines of England', in Esther M. Morgan-Ellis and Kay Norton, eds, *The Oxford Handbook of Community Singing* (Oxford: Oxford University Press, 2024), pp. 161–182.

Schafer, R. Murray, *The Soundscape: Our Sonic Environment and the Tuning of the World* (Rochester, Vermont: Destiny Books, 1994).

Schoonderwoerd, Pieter, '"Shall We Sing a Song for You?": Mediation, Migration and Identity in Football Chants and Fandom', *Soccer & Society*, 12:1 (2010), 120–141. https://doi.org/10.1080/14660970.2011.530482.

Scriptor, 'Manchester 1938', *Comradeship*, 29: 3 (Spring 1938), 9–11.

Secord, Anne, 'Science in the Pub: Artisan Botanists in Early Nineteenth-Century Lancashire', *History of Science*, 32: 97 (1994), 269–315.

Sellers, Christopher, 'To Place or Not to Place: Toward an Environmental History of Modern Medicine', *Bulletin of the History of Medicine*, 92: 1 (2018), 1–45.

Sheppard, Jennifer, 'Sound of Body: Music, Sports and Health in Victorian Britain', *Journal of the Royal Musical Association*, 140: 2 (2015), 343–369.

Sidgwick, Arthur H., *Walking Essays* (London: Edward Arnold, 1922).

Sissons, Dave, Howard, Terry and Smith, Roly, *Clarion Call: Sheffield's Access Pioneers* (Sheffield: Clarion Call Editorial Group, 2017).

Sissons, David, *A Sheffield Clarion Rambler: Some Aspects of the Life and Work of G. H. B. Ward (1876–1957)*, (University of Sheffield: Unpublished MA Thesis, 1992).

Smith, Mark, *The Sensory Manifesto* (University Park: Penn State University Press, 2021).

Snape, Robert, 'The Co-operative Holidays Association and the Cultural Formation of Countryside Leisure Practice', *Leisure Studies*, 23: 2 (2004), 143–158.

Spinney, Justin, 'Close Encounters? Mobile Methods, (Post)phenomenology and Affect', *Cultural Geographies*, 22: 2 (2015), 231–246.

Stimpson, J. A., 'Musical memories of Totnes', *Comradeship*, 40:2 (Winter 1948), p. 3.

Stocker, Michael, *Hear Where We Are: Sound, Ecology and Sense of Place* (New York: Springer, 2013).

Taylor, Harvey, *A Claim on the Countryside: A History of the British Outdoor Movement* (Edinburgh: Edinburgh University Press, 1997).

Taylor, Lisa and Whalley, Boff, '"Real Change Comes from below!": Walking and Singing about Places that Matter; the Formation of Commoners Choir', *Leisure Studies*, 38:1 (2019), 58–73.

Tebbutt, Melanie, 'Rambling and Manly Identity in Derbyshire's Dark Peak, 1880s–1920s', *The Historical Journal* 49: 4 (2006), 1125–1153.

The Co-operative Holiday Association, *Summer Holidays in the Isle of Man (Peel). Programme, Songs Etc.* London: CHA, 1938. Sheffield City Archive X95 2007/42.

The Co-operative Holiday Association and The Holiday Fellowship, *Songs of Faith, Nature and Fellowship* (London: CHA and HF, 1951). National Co-operative Archive, GB 1499 CHA /3/2.

The Holiday Fellowship, *Songs by the Way* (tunebook) (London: Holiday Fellowship, 1923).

The Holiday Fellowship, *Songs by the Way* (London: Holiday Fellowship, n.d.).

The Holiday Fellowship, *Fellowship Holidays: Programme & Songs* (The Holiday Fellowship, 1929). Co-operative Heritage Trust, CHA/2/1.

The Mountain Club, *The Mountain Club Songbook* (self published, 1955). Vaughan Williams Memorial Library, MP 30.6.

The Wee Mon, 'Our Coming of Age Ramble, September 4th 1921', *Sheffield Clarion Ramblers Handbook 2022–23*, 56–60.

Theorell, Töres, *Psychological Health Effects of Musical Experiences Theories, Studies and Reflections in Music Health Science* (SpringerBriefs in Psychology, 2014).

Tilley, Christopher, *A Phenomenology of Landscape: Places, Paths and Monuments* (Oxford: Berg, 1994).

Tilley, Christopher and Cameron-Daum, Kate, *An Anthropology of Landscape: The Extraordinary in the Ordinary* (London: UCL Press, 2017).

Turner, Edith, *Communitas: The Anthropology of Collective Joy* (New York: Palgrave Macmillan, 2012).

Twidle, Hedley and Elaff, Aragorn, 'Sounding Environments', in Emily O'Gorman, William San Martín, Mark Carey and Sandra Swart, eds, *The Routledge Handbook of Environmental History* (1st ed.) (London: Routledge, 2023), 49–65.

von Hardenberg, Wilko Graf and Fehl, Anne, 'Environmental Echoes: Finding Historical Soundscapes of Nature in Textual Sources', *Journal of Literature and Science*, 17: 2 (2024), pp. 73–92.

Waddington, Keir, '"In a Country Every Way by Nature Favourable to Health": Landscape and Public Health in Victorian Rural Wales', *Canadian Bulletin of Medical History*, 31: 2 (2014), 183–204.

Wainwright, Megan, 'Sensing the Airs: The Cultural Context for Breathing and Breathlessness in Uruguay', *Medical Anthropology*, 36: 4 (2017), 332–347.

Walford Davies, Henry, 'Our new songbook', *Comradeship*, 9:1 (1915), 9–10.

Walford Davies, Henry, *The Fellowship Songbook* (Liverpool: Rushworth and Dreaper, 1915).

'Wanderbird', 'A new invasion of the hills', *Northern Rambler*, 1:1 (October 1935), 6.

Ward, George H. B., 'Ramblers all: Zest, health and joy', *Sheffield Clarion Ramblers Handbook 1921–22*, pp. 58–61.

Ward, George Herbert Bridges, *Songs for Ramblers to Sing on the Moorlands* (Sheffield: Sheffield Clarion Ramblers, 1922).

Ward, G. H. B., '"Foreign" S.C.R. members', *Sheffield Clarion Ramblers Handbook 1949–50*, pp. 67–68.

Ward, G. H. B., 'Three men of the moors', *Sheffield Clarion Ramblers Handbook 1949–50*, p. 83.

Ward, G. H. B., 'Vandalism in paradise', *Sheffield Clarion Ramblers Handbook 1950–51*, 176–179.

Ward, G. H. B., 'The rambler and "hiker"', *Sheffield Clarion Ramblers Handbook 1951–52*, pp. 67–70.

Ward, G. H. B., 'Brazen Blackpool', *Sheffield Clarion Ramblers Handbook 1954–55*, pp. 68-69.

Ward, G. H. B. 'Motor cyclists "access"', *Sheffield Clarion Ramblers Handbook 1955–56*, pp. 121–123.

Warrender, Keith, *Forbidden Kinder: The 1932 Mass Trespass Re-visited* (Timperley: Willow, 2022).

Wicks, Sidney F. 'A Reverie', in Manchester Ramblers' Federation, *The Rambler's Handbook 1927*: 14–15.

Wild, Harold E., 'The unobtrusive rambler', in Manchester Ramblers' Federation, *The Rambler's Handbook 1928*: 29–30, p. 30.

Wright, Mr. 'A contemporary holiday association', *CHA Magazine*, 57: 1 (Summer 1966), 5–7.

Zweiniger-Bargielowska, Ina, *Managing the Body: Beauty, Health, and Fitness in Britain, 1880–1939* (Oxford: Oxford University Press, 2010).

Acknowledgements

Many thanks to the Co-operative Heritage Trust, Sheffield City Archives and Local Studies Library, Manchester Libraries, Information and Archives, the Working Class Movement Library, the Vaughan Williams Memorial Library, the British Library, and Derbyshire Records Office for access to archival material, and to members of Lakeland Voice for generously sharing their experiences.

This work was carried out as part of the *In All Our Footsteps* project, funded by the UK Arts and Humanities Research Council (grant number AH/V00509X/1) https://www.allourfootsteps.uk/

The qualitative research reported on in this Element received ethical approval from Newcastle University.

Cambridge Elements

Histories of Emotions and the Senses

Series Editors

Rob Boddice
Tampere University

Rob Boddice (PhD, FRHistS) is Senior Research Fellow at the Academy of Finland Centre of Excellence in the History of Experiences. He is the author/editor of thirteen books, including *Knowing Pain: A History of Sensation, Emotion and Experience* (Polity Press, 2023), *Humane Professions: The Defence of Experimental Medicine, 1876–1914* (Cambridge University Press, 2021) and *A History of Feelings* (Reaktion, 2019).

Piroska Nagy
Université du Québec à Montréal (UQAM)

Piroska Nagy is Professor of Medieval History at the Université du Québec à Montréal (UQAM) and initiated the first research program in French on the history of emotions. She is the author or editor of fourteen volumes, including *Le Don des larmes au Moyen Âge* (Albin Michel, 2000); *Medieval Sensibilities: A History of Emotions in the Middle Ages*, with Damien Boquet (Polity, 2018); and *Histoire des émotions collectives: Épistémologie, émergences*, expériences, with D. Boquet and L. Zanetti Domingues (Classiques Garnier, 2022).

Mark Smith
University of South Carolina

Mark Smith (PhD, FRHistS) is Carolina Distinguished Professor of History and Director of the Institute for Southern Studies at the University of South Carolina. He is author or editor of over a dozen books and his work has been translated into Chinese, Korean, Danish, German, and Spanish. He has lectured in Europe, throughout the United States, Australia, and China and his work has been featured in the New York Times, the London Times, the Washington Post, and the Wall Street Journal. He serves on the US Commission for Civil Rights.

About the Series

Born of the emotional and sensory "turns", Elements in Histories of Emotions and the Senses move one of the fastest-growing interdisciplinary fields forward. The series is aimed at scholars across the humanities, social sciences, and life sciences, embracing insights from a diverse range of disciplines, from neuroscience to art history and economics. Chronologically and regionally broad, encompassing global, transnational, and deep history, it concerns such topics as affect theory, intersensoriality, embodiment, human–animal relations, and distributed cognition. The founding editor of the series was Jan Plamper.

Cambridge Elements

Histories of Emotions and the Senses

Elements in the Series

Memes, History and Emotional Life
Katie Barclay and Leanne Downing

Boredom
Elena Carrera

Marketing Violence: The Affective Economy of Violent Imageries in the Dutch Republic
Frans-Willem Korsten, Inger Leemans, Cornelis van der Haven, and Karel Vanhaesebrouck

Beyond Compassion: Gender and Humanitarian Action
Dolores Martín-Moruno

Uncertainty and Emotion in the 1900 Sydney Plague
Philippa Nicole Barr

Sensorium: Contextualizing the Senses and Cognition in History and Across Cultures
David Howes

Zionism: Emotions, Language, and Experience
Ofer Idels

Affective Touching: Neurobiology and Technological Applications
Mark Paterson

Embodied Epistemology as Rigorous Historical Method
Lauren Mancia

Making Sense of Knowledge: Feminist Epistemologies in the Greek Birth Control Movement (1974–1986)
Evangelia (Lina) Chordaki

Disenchanting the Senses: Sulfuric Discourse and the World System
Andrew Kettler

Outdoor Singing in Modern Britain: A Sensory and Emotional History
Abbi Flint and Clare Hickman

A full series listing is available at: www.cambridge.org/EHES

For EU product safety concerns, contact us at Calle de José Abascal, 56–1°,
28003 Madrid, Spain or eugpsr@cambridge.org.

www.ingramcontent.com/pod-product-compliance
Lightning Source LLC
LaVergne TN
LVHW011854060526
838200LV00054B/4328